More MURDER, M... and MAYH... BIRKENH... including Wallasey and New Brighton

By David Malcolm and Ian Boumphrey

Published by
Ian & Marilyn Boumphrey
The Nook
7 Acrefield Road
Prenton
Wirral L42 8LD

Design & Origination
Ian Boumphrey

Printed by
Eaton Press Ltd
Westfield Road
Wallasey
Wirral L44 7JB

ISBN 1 899241 09 4

Price
£5.95

CONTENTS

ACKNOWLEDGEMENTS

We would like to thank the following for their help and support in publishing this book: Mr Tony Mossman - Curator of the Merseyside Police Library and Museum, the staff of Wirral Borough Libraries for their willing and gracious assistance, the Liverpool Post and Echo for access to their library and picture archives, Bob Bird for his photographs, Ken Tait for the shipping photographs, The Daily Mirror, Lever Bros & Port Sunlight Heritage, the many, now retired, members of the local police force too numerous to mention individually but an especial thanks to Jack Hastie and John Slater, and to Albert Nute for his assistance.

INTRODUCTION

The events in this, the second book detailing true-life stories of murder, mayhem and mystery in Birkenhead and including the Wallasey area, are based on authentic original research into police files, court proceedings and newspaper reports. They span a period of almost sixty years - a period when the penalty for the crime of murder was death by hanging, unless that sentence was commuted to life imprisonment by the Monarch acting on the recommendation of the Home Secretary.

The first chapter of this book deals with the 1955 Pill Box Murder in Woodchurch, which remains unsolved to this day. It was in this year that Ruth Ellis, the last woman sentenced to death in this country, faced the gallows to a huge outcry from the general public. There had been miscarriages of justice before 1955 notably in the case of Timothy Evans and the disturbing outcome of the Craig case. Ten years later the death sentence had been completely abolished. Did the abolition of the death penalty have any effect on the murder rate on the Wirral? It would appear not as the annual figures for this, the most malevolent of crimes, are stable from the time that records are available in 1843 to the present time.

These are not ordinary crimes - murder is the ultimate act. It is a crime which has a far-reaching effect on the victims' families, the families of the perpetrator and indeed on the whole community, living on long after the crime has been committed. Responsibility often becomes shared. "If only I had done . . . . perhaps this would not have happened," is a common response to this heinous crime. The motives displayed in these events are varied. There is always anger. There may be greed and jealousy, all-possessing love or thwarted love. Fear and desperation may result in the urge to kill another human being. Any of these feelings may be enough taken to the extreme to tip the scales of rationality of the human mind.

Murder is the ultimate horror. It can happen to rich or poor, young or old. It is a horror which has been reduced by overexposure on television and in the cinema. The effect on our minds of the real horror of the crime and the terror of the victims has been numbed by constant repetition until we sometimes no longer react to it as an evil crime; a crime from which there is no return, no going back. Perhaps in reading this book and letting your own imagination fill in the scene you can appreciate the terror of the final moments. The events in this book tell us something about the perpetrators and their victims. Perhaps they will tell us something about our inner selves and the human condition.

Chapter one

THE PILLBOX MURDER

T he 24 September 1955 was a Saturday, which was great as far as 11 year old Peter Williams was concerned. He did not have to go to school. It was not that he did not like Grange Secondary School but he looked forward to the weekends when he and his friends could explore the fields of the Fender valley and let their imaginations run riot. But this particular Saturday had not started very well. His mother had given him his breakfast but by the time he was ready to go out it was raining.

Peter Williams stared gloomily out of the window of 19 Walby Close as the rain continued to fall. He was bored. It was now 10 o'clock; his father was at work and would not be home until late and his mother was busy in the kitchen. He had nothing to do. If only the rain would stop he could meet his friends, Sidney Smith and Brian Lemon. They had seen some blackberry bushes the other day along the side of the railway track which ran by a narrow stream optimistically called the River Fender. As soon as the rain stopped he would call for them and they would go across the fields, cross the small bridge over the river then along the embankment and see how many blackberries they could collect.

As he looked down the close he noticed the sky lightening and within minutes the sun had broken through the cloud. It was going to be a great day after all. Peter called through to the kitchen to tell his mother that he was off and as he left the house he yelled, "Bye, Mum. I'll bring you back some blackberries," and raced off down the road to find Brian and Sidney. The three boys made their way light-heartedly through the quickly drying grass of the Fender Valley to the little bridge over the stream, crossed over and turned to their left to work their way along the embankment of the Seacombe to Wrexham railway line. About 100 yards further along between the stream and the railway line was an old disused army pillbox which had originally

The Pillbox Murder

been built to defend Prenton from the German hordes in the Second World War. Built of concrete in the standard shape, with the doorway on the north side, it had seen service only for Home Guard training. No door existed now, ten years after the war, and it was a favourite, if spooky, place for the boys to play. As they moved slowly along the embankment picking the berries and stuffing them into their handkerchiefs the boys became separated as they approached the pillbox with Brian and Sid passing behind the pillbox between it and the railway line while Peter decided to go round the front. As he crept past the open doorway of the pillbox and peered into the gloomy depths he was surprised to see what he thought were the feet and legs of a tailor's dummy. He could not see very clearly so he stepped gingerly inside and touched one of the feet.

"It must be a dummy," he thought. "It hasn't got any toes! This could be a bit of a laugh. What I'll do is take one of the legs and creep round the pillbox and wave it at the other boys and frighten them." But as Peter started to lift the leg he realised that it did not appear to have any toes because it was a human leg covered with a thick stocking. And as he peered

A view from the pillbox with the distant houses in Woodchurch Road, by Prenton Bridge, and the Seacombe - Wrexham railway line on the left

further into the gloom he saw that the legs were attached to a body which had been loosely covered with old clothes.

Suddenly Peter was scared. He ran yelling out of the pillbox. "What's the matter?" shouted Brian, but he did not get a reply as Peter leapt over the stream and hared across the fields. Brian and Sid ran after him but Peter was far ahead and did not hear their enquiring cries. Peter raced into the house to tell his mother but by the time he got there he was so out-of-breathe and confused that his mother could not make any sense of what he was trying to tell her. She could not believe this strange story that her son was blurting out. Was it all one of Peter's make-believe games?

Peter knew that someone had to tell the police and he knew that there were two policemen who lived nearby. He dashed out of the house and hammered on their door. There was no answer. What should he do now? He was a bit calmer as he made his way back home again and by now his mother seemed to have taken him seriously. She was out in New Hey Road looking for him and talking to the Birkenhead Co-operative Society milk-roundsman. "Tell the milkman what you told me," she said and Peter told his story again. "You'd better take me over there now and show me what you found," said the milkman, despite being in the middle of his round. By this time Brian and Sid had arrived back and the four set off back across the fields to the pillbox. Brian and Sid soon fell behind and as they approached the stream Peter too stayed back; he did not want to go near the pillbox ever again.

The milkman continued on to the pillbox, peered inside for a minute and as his eyes became accustomed to the dark saw, as Peter had done, a female body wearing only stockings and the upper body obscured by a pile of clothing. He turned in the doorway to look back at Peter. "My God, you were right!" he shouted.

As they were walking the quarter mile or so back across the fields two burly policemen were arriving at the Williams' house in response to a telephone call made by Mrs Williams. Peter had recovered somewhat by then, helped by the kindly presence of the milkman, but on arrival back in Walby Close he was, like any small boy, frightened stiff by the sight of the policemen standing outside his house especially as one shouted on seeing him, "That's him." Peter was sure that they thought he was responsible for

The Pillbox Murder

A train on the Seacombe to Wrexham line passes the pill box, watched by a policeman.

the dead body in the pill box.

On being reassured by the policemen that they were only relieved that he had come home and that he had done nothing wrong the policemen went back into the house to telephone Detective Chief Inspector MacIntosh, the head of Birkenhead CID at that time, who immediately arranged for the Chief Constable, Mr HJ Vann and his Deputy, Superintendent Tankard, to meet him at the deserted pillbox. After a short consultation the three men decided that they had a murder enquiry on their hands and that not only would they require all the resources of Birkenhead CID but also that it would be necessary to enlist the help of the other local forces, notably Wallasey and Cheshire County Police. Detective Inspector Dave Smith was the first to arrive at the scene followed shortly afterwards by Detective Constable Jack Joinson (later to become Detective-Inspector in charge of Birkenhead CID). Dog teams from Lancashire County and Liverpool police forces were brought in to go over the fields for clues and to try to pick up any scents. Mine-detection equipment was also ordered to comb the fields around the pillbox for any items which might help to identify the body or the killer. Dr Charles A St Hill, the Home Office Pathologist for the area, was called immediately as was Dr JB Firth from the Forensic Science Laboratory at Preston. In this way began the most extensive and complex murder inquiry in the history of Birkenhead.

Dr St Hill's initial examination in the pillbox revealed that the body was that of a woman who appeared to be aged 50 to 60, about 5ft 2ins tall with grey eyes, greying hair, no teeth and hair around her chin and mouth. She was of slight build and was not wearing a wedding ring. The clothing which had been left piled on her naked body consisted of a lemon coloured linen two-piece suit with glass buttons and no belt, green leather, badly worn, court shoes with high heels, black suede gloves and a dark brown herringbone tweed coat. Two pieces of underclothing were also found placed on top of the body. All were of poor quality.

Death appeared to have been caused by strangulation, apparently with a belt or possibly the strap of a handbag; neither the handbag nor any type of belt were ever found. Some sort of sharp instrument had been used to mutilate the body - probably a knife - but this was nowhere to be found.

The Pillbox Murder

The next problem was to find out the identity of the body.

Police cars with loud hailers were sent out to tour the town broadcasting the woman's description and asking, "Is any woman in your road missing?" And house-to-house enquiries were started in Woodchurch, Upton and Moreton, coordinated by DCI McIntosh and DI Harry Lang, head of Wallasey CID, from the nerve centre at Moreton Police Station.

Extensive searching of the area around the pillbox revealed little to help the police but inside the pillbox were found a lipstick which had been used to write obscenities on her body (something which was not revealed to the public at that time) and a copy of the Daily Mirror newspaper dated 21 September 1955, in which some horses racing that day at Brighton had been underlined in red ink and part of another page had been torn out. There had been little bleeding from the mutilations but samples of blood-caked dirt were obtained which were taken back to the Forensic Science Laboratory by Dr Firth together with the lipstick, the newspaper and the clothing. The body was removed at 4.30pm that afternoon to the Birkenhead mortuary where Dr St Hill prepared to perform a complete postmortem.

Dr St Hill estimated that the victim had been dead for two or three days. There was an elongated bruise about two inches long beneath the point of the jaw, bruising to the upper lip extending into her mouth and her lip was lacerated. A deep severe bruise was present on the back of the skull and there was bruising to the right side of the head. Her wrists and arms showed extensive scratch marks. There was a deep laceration over the large toe joint of the left foot which had been caused by the ill-fitting second-hand shoes the deceased had worn. In Dr St Hill's opinion this would have been extremely painful and might have caused a pronounced limp. Around the neck was a linear, band-like, abraded and bruised mark consistent with the use of a belt. The cause of death was asphyxia due to strangulation.

Furthermore, the post mortem provided some rather unusual results. There was a vertical incision 12 inches long in her abdomen which nowadays would have no doubt excited criminal psychologists with its Freudian connotations, and another 4 inch incision at the base of her right buttock running parallel with the vaginal and rectal orifices. Both of these incisions appeared to have been caused by a sharp penknife after her death, which accounted for the lack of blood on the floor of the pillbox. Intercourse had taken place just before death and examination of the vagina showed a small clean incision in the wall of the vagina and a stab-like wound near the mouth of the uterus. Obscene words had been scrawled across the chest of the deceased and on the left thigh. These letters had been done by gouging out the lipstick with a knife and then smearing the skin with it. This again was something that was kept from the general public.

Forensic examination concentrated on the clothing which revealed that the inside and outside of the coat showed eight pieces of twin strand clockwise twist threads, royal blue in colour, adhering to the material. Two similar threads were on the skirt, whilst in the finger nail scrapings were more identical blue threads. Dr Firth suggested that the fibres may have come from a royal blue pullover or similar garment. The lipstick showed that a knife had been used as suggested by Dr St Hill to gouge out the top. Samples of the blood stained dirt were unable to give any information as to blood type and the newspaper did not reveal any usable fingerprints or fibre samples. This process took a week during which the police were without what might have proved to be a vital clue - that of the torn-out part of the newspaper.

A full-face photo of the victim, Alice Barton, superimposed on a photo of a dressed dummy - used in local newspapers to identify the body (see next page)

In many of the major murder enquiries of the 1950s Scotland Yard were called in and on the following Monday, 26 September, the Chief Constable officially requested their assistance. Detective Superintendent George 'Dusty' Miller and Detective Sergeant Ernest Bellamy arrived by train from London at 4.30pm and immediately set to work.

A macabre after-death composite photograph of the victim was published in the Liverpool Daily Post and later in the Birkenhead News. This was done by dressing a tailor's dummy in the deceased clothes with a post mortem photograph of the full face superimposed; an idea which was considered novel at the time (*see opposite page*).

Police identification took some days but piecing together the jigsaw puzzle of her life took much longer. By the early hours of Tuesday morning 27 September a partial identification was obtained through Mr John Robinson of Liverpool. He had seen the composite photograph in the Daily Post and had volunteered to come over to Birkenhead mortuary where he felt reasonably certain that the body was that of Alice Barton, who had lived with him as his housekeeper from December 1954 until March 1955. Enquiries were made about Alice Barton, nee Davies, and it was discovered that she was born at Wigan on 10 April 1906 and on 19 March 1927 had married John Barton at the Wigan Register Office. John Barton, who still lived in Atherton, near Wigan, was contacted and he attended the mortuary on the evening of 27 September, but he was unable to make a positive identification, saying that he had not seen his wife for over ten years.

The following morning, however, a positive identification was given by George Kendrick, a Liverpool labourer, who had lived with Alice Barton from May 1955 until early September. He told the police that she had spoken of having a husband and one son, and that in the past she had lived in Huddersfield, Bristol and Wigan. On 29 September John Barton was again interviewed and made a further visit to the mortuary when he made a more definite identification. Perhaps Mr Barton felt too ashamed to identify his wife on the first occasion and also in his thoughts may have been the effect that it would have on Alice Barton's illegitimate son, who he had accepted as his own.

At last the police were satisfied as to the identity of the body and on the following day, 30 September 1955, the body of Alice Barton was taken to the Church of England Chapel at Landican Cemetery where a funeral service was held and her body laid to rest. There was only one mourner at the funeral; the small, solitary, bowed figure of John Barton. On the coffin were two wreaths made of white, purple and mauve dahlias; both from her husband, one bearing the inscription, 'To my dear wife. Lie in peace. All forgiven. From your loving husband. Jack.' And the other inscribed, 'To Alice. In loving memory. Jack.' Outside more than a hundred people had gathered to watch and mingling with the crowd were Detective Chief Inspector MacIntosh and the two Scotland Yard detectives who had come to see if anyone fitted the description they had been given of someone who had been seen in Alice Barton's company on that fatal day just over a week before. They were looking for 'a man aged between 35 and 45, about 5ft 6ins tall, with black hair, a clear complexion, long nose, dark eyebrows, clean-shaven with a pointed chin and of unkempt appearance.'

By this time the police had built up a comprehensive picture of Alice Barton. After her marriage she had lived with her husband at 637 Atherton Road, Hindley Green near Wigan and during the early years of the Second World War, she had worked in a munitions factory near Chorley, Lancashire. She began associating with other men and as a consequence of this she gave birth to an illegitimate son on 29 October 1943. Mr Barton registered the child as legitimate, naming himself as the father but Alice would have nothing to do with the child and continued to visit public houses and associate with other men. The couple argued constantly about the child but Alice would not mend her ways. Her attitude was summed up in one of her outbursts. "Put the brat in the Infirmary," she had shouted at her husband. By December 1943 the trouble between them had reached fever pitch and on Christmas Eve Alice Barton walked out of the house and was not seen again by her husband until he saw her body on a mortuary slab on 27 September 1955.

Further investigation into the history of Alice Barton showed that she had lived with a Mr Francis Foster in Mold Green, Huddersfield from 1947 to early 1949, when she left him without any apparent reason. Early in 1950 she turned up in Bristol and there lived with Mr Frederick Cooke in Saltford. Later that year Cooke committed suicide. At that time Alice Barton was well established in a life of prostitution. Her appearance was described as filthy and when she had any money she spent it all on drink. During the latter part of 1952 she resided with Mr George Canlin at Lydney Road, Southmead, and Arlington Villas. She also did a little housework for a Mr Edward Pearce of Jacobs Wells Buildings, who later reported that he often missed little sums of money from his room while she was employed by him.

She suddenly deserted George Canlin at the end of August 1954 and took to the roads with Frederick Bathe, a known criminal. They roamed the countryside together until 8 September 1954 when Barton was arrested at Lyneham, Wiltshire, as being 'identical with a woman named Alice Barton wanted for larceny from a house in Stockport'. She was taken to Stockport by police escort but on being interviewed there about the offence she denied any responsibility. Among her few belongings at the time of her arrest was a piece of paper bearing an address in Wallasey, but unfortunately neither the officers at Stockport or Lyneham made a note of it. Witnesses were unable to identify her and so she was released and placed on a bus to Manchester.

For almost three months Alice Barton disappeared from sight; although it was known that she went to Manchester the police were unable to trace her movements in that city. The next sighting was in Liverpool in early December when she was seen at the Quadrant coffee stall in Lime Street. The stall was situated quite near to the mouth of the Mersey Tunnel, opposite the entrance to Lime Street Station and less than half a mile from the Pierhead. It was open all night and much frequented by the local prostitutes, thieves and vagrants amongst whom was Ronald Thompson *alias* Swaine, a petty criminal who also arranged the hire of taxicabs for prostitutes and their clients. He it was who claimed that Alice Barton arrived in Liverpool in December and it is certain that she was plying her trade between Lime Street and the Pierhead in that month. Just before Christmas she met a 63 year old bargeman, John Robinson, in the *Liverpool Arms* public house, better known as *Tom Hall's*, in Water Street, Liverpool and moved in with him as his housekeeper. John Robinson did provide the police with some useful pieces of information. He was adamant that when she came to live with him she only had the clothes she stood up in and a brown bag with a few personal items. He was also certain that she did not have any teeth and that he never saw her with dentures.

During the first few months of 1955 she was a familiar sight at the Crosville Cafe at the Pierhead, sitting quietly in a corner, arms across her chest, not soliciting her customers but waiting patiently to be asked for her services.

She became well known there and after she left Robinson often slept rough at the Pier Head. Thomas McCormick saw her frequently in the Crosville Cafe and introduced her to George Kendrick, a man with a criminal record and described by Detective Superintendent Miller as a 'most repulsive man of the lowest type'. On 25 May 1955 Kendrick, who had lived on public assistance for years, applied to the National Assistance Board for additional benefit for Mrs Alice Barton, who was 'staying with him and caring for him'. They were then living in Aubrey Street, Liverpool, and she was granted a payment of £1 a week.

Though they were living together, Alice Barton spent most of her time at the Pier Head and her old haunts, the public houses and cafes from Lime Street down to the river. By June she had extended her area to Bootle where she frequented the *Royal*, *Caradoc* and *St Winifred's* public houses. This was no doubt due to the fact that Kendrick, who walked with a stick, had taken to following her about the Liverpool area, where he was often to be seen arguing with her and brandishing his walking stick at her. It was about this time that she purchased the lemon coloured suit from a second-hand stall in 'Paddy's Market' together with some second-hand green shoes. Kendrick supplied another piece of the jigsaw; he was positive that the suit had no belt.

Alice Barton left Aubrey Street at the beginning of August and again slept rough at the Pier Head or, if she was in Bootle in the evenings, she stayed the night on Seaforth Sands. Her practice in the evenings was to sit in a Bootle public house, purchase a half pint of mild ale and make her own cigarettes from ends picked up in the street. These she had in a tin which she kept in a small brown leather shopping bag, which she carried folded under her arm. She was a pathetic, masculine looking creature who people took pity on and brought her drinks, tea and food, in addition to giving her money. Somehow or other she nearly always managed to return to the Crosville Cafe around 7am, probably by way of the old Overhead Railway, and was usually seen there again around 4pm to 5pm.

One week before her death she met Kendrick at the Pier Head and they visited 'Paddy's Market' once more, where she purchased a brown tweed coat. She slept with Kendrick on the nights of the 14 and 15 September, but left him during that day. Kendrick had assaulted her many times before but it was noticed by the habitués of the Crosville Cafe that she had a black eye that day. He may have been an ugly and violent man but he was obviously still virile as police enquiries discovered; he slept with three different prostitutes in the four days before Barton left! The next few days saw her around her old haunts again. Kendrick tried to assault her in the Crosville Cafe on the 18 September and a police officer had to be called to stop the affray. John Robinson saw her on the 19 September at the Pier Head at 7.30am and again that afternoon at about 4.30pm when he noticed that she was limping. That night she undoubtedly slept on the sands at Seaforth, because she was seen in the snack bar at the Seaforth Sands Overhead railway station by the proprietor, John Beck, and his daughter, June, at 10am on Tuesday 20 September. The bar staff, at the *St Winifred's* public house in Bootle, Johanna Clarke, Margaret Crichton and William Tracey, recognised her as she entered the pub at around noon and there she stayed until closing time at 3pm.

Meanwhile an event occurred which was to use up an enormous amount of police time and manpower. On the morning of the 20 September the *S.S. Empress of France* arrived in the Gladstone Dock nearby and most of the crew were free of the ship by 2pm. A few of them drifted into the *St Winifred's* but nobody saw Alice Barton speak to, or leave with, anyone. Later that afternoon she was seen alone in the Crosville Cafe by Irene Decker *alias* Hardacre, a convicted prostitute, from Grove Street, Liverpool, and again about 10.30pm at the Quadrant coffee stall where she was talking to another vagrant, Marie Hammond. A little later Decker saw Alice Barton get into a car with a young man. Ronald Thompson also saw the event and identified the person in question as a man who had been a fellow prisoner in Walton Prison in 1952 by the name of Roy Ellison, aged 28, from Preston. When questioned later Ellison denied all knowledge of seeing or talking to Alice Barton but this may have been wariness of the police on his part as investigation confirmed his alibi for the following day.

The 21 September, the day of Alice Barton's death, dawned dull and cold with a stiff, sharp breeze blowing across the River Mersey. Mrs Barbara Shaw was at work early that day as usual in Finlay's tobacco kiosk on the landing stage. As she looked out of the small kiosk she recognised Alice

The Pillbox Murder

Barton walking along the landing stage towards the Woodside ferry boat. The time, she thought, was "about quarter to nine." This was confirmed by Harry Sayle, of Wallasey, a second engineer on the tug *Fighting Cock*. He knew Alice Barton by sight having seen her at *Tom Hall's* and in the ornamental gardens at Pier Head. It was 9am as Harry Sayle watched Alice Barton board the ferry. By 9.30am it had begun to rain and it kept on raining incessantly until just after noon. In the thin, inadequate clothes she was wearing Alice Barton must have been cold and wet and a very unprepossessing sight.

Bann's Market stood among a group of shops at Moreton Cross. The shop assistant, Isabella Sherlock, was busy that Wednesday morning but not too busy to notice a bedraggled, dirty, old-looking woman who came into the shop about 10am to ask if she had any cheap bananas to sell. Feeling sorry for her Mrs Sherlock gave the dejected-looking woman a pound and a half of poor quality bananas for the sixpence proffered to her. Later she was to recognise the customer as Alice Barton and certainly the post mortem confirmed that the dead woman had ingested bananas as her last meal.

Marjorie Bunney, Mary Dollard and Mary Platt, all of Moreton, also saw Barton at Moreton Cross but Kenneth Sparrow, a bus driver, was sure that he had seen her at about the same time, standing outside the *Coach and*

The No 77 bus collected Alice Barton and the unknown man from a bus stop on the right in Upton Road Moreton and took them to Arrowe Park.
(This photo was taken a few years after the event)

Horses public house with a man aged between 35 and 45, wearing a dirty raincoat.

What was Alice Barton doing in Moreton that day? Later investigation showed that this appeared to be the only time that Barton had crossed the river to the Wirral side; no one ever reported seeing her in Wirral except on this occasion. Had she made a special journey to Moreton to meet someone she knew from her past? Or had she come to meet a special client? It seems doubtful that she would have made the long and, to her, expensive journey by ferry and bus to Moreton on the chance of doing business.

The number 77 bus had very few people on board as it pulled in to the compulsory stop on the opposite side of the roundabout to the *Coach and Horses* on its way from Moreton Shore to Birkenhead (*see previous page*). About eight to ten people boarded the bus which was on schedule at 10.17am. One of the boarders was Alice Barton, followed by a man, described as wearing a dirty raincoat. Barton mounted the stairs to the upper deck, whilst the other passengers, with the exception of the man, entered the lower deck. As the man went to follow Barton up the stairs he tapped the conductress, Lilian Martindale, on the shoulder and said, "Two to Arrowe Park." He offered her sixpence and she in return gave him two threepenny tickets. The fare for this stage had been raised from 2½d to 3d (1p) in 1953. The man appeared not to expect any change as he continued on to the upper deck. Did this mean that the man was a local and that he had used this bus service before? If not, how had he known the correct fare? Or was it just coincidence?

Mrs Martindale visited the upper deck on several occasions during the journey; the man and the woman were sitting on the rear seat deep in earnest conversation. The couple alighted at the stop at the side of the *Arrowe Park Hotel* and the observant Mrs Martindale noted as the bus drew away that the woman was 'adjusting her dress'. Neither of them was seen again until between 11.20am and 11.25am when they tried to enter the buffet bar of the *Arrowe Park Hotel*. The head man, Cecil John McLeavy, was cleaning the windows. Sarah Kerrigan and Mary Williams were working inside the bar preparing for the first customers of the day. Mr McLeavy called to the couple, "We won't be a second, it's not opening time yet," which provoked

The Arrowe Park Hotel as it looked in 1955, with the Park entrance on the left

an odd response from the man. "What time do you close?" he asked, "3pm" was McLeavy's reply. Surely if the man had been from Birkenhead he would have known when closing time was; perhaps he was from Wallasey or even Moreton where the public houses opened at 11am and closed at 2.30pm. At that time bar opening and closing times were in the hands of the local authority and varied considerably from area to area.

The official opening time arrived at 11.30am and Sarah Kerrigan asked the couple, who were the only people in the pub, what they would like and the man approached the counter. Alice Barton remained seated behind a small glass partition in the bar. "I'll have a Guinness, a port and a glass of bitter," said the man, taking a one pound note from his back trouser pocket. Sarah inadvertently gave him change for a ten shilling note but the man did not notice and took the drinks back to the corner of the bar where Alice was sitting. She drank the Guinness and port and he was merely sipping at his glass of bitter when he realised he had been given the wrong change. He rose, moved over to the bar and politely asked Sarah if she had made a mistake which she checked in the till and rectified immediately. Alice Barton stayed in the corner and said nothing but one thing the girls did notice was that the woman was wearing lipstick heavily smeared across her lips - seldom did Alice Barton use lipstick according to those who knew her.

The man continued to remain on his feet as he maintained a conversation with the three bar staff. He bought drinks on two further occasions and also some cigarettes, walking around the bar all the time. Sarah and Mary thought him a bit of a swaggering, boastful type and rather strange. He claimed that he was a coach owner who had made a pile of money during the railway strike, running his coach between Ramsgate and Margate. Also, he had been in hospital for twelve months, during which time he had loaned his coach to someone else who had ruined it by slashing the seats. "I know who is responsible," he said, "and I'll get my revenge." Mr McLeavy watched them as they left the hotel at 12.30pm. What a strange couple, he thought, as they disappeared through the main gates into Arrowe Park.

William Carroll was on his rounds as a Park Constable when he heard voices emanating from one of two cubicles in the male toilets behind the children's playground. The door of the first cubicle was shut but not locked. He pushed hard. There was considerable resistance but finally he managed to push the door open and was confronted by the sight of a woman, fully dressed, with her back to the door, and a man facing her. The man was fastening his trousers. Mr Carroll demanded to know what they were doing and ordered them out of the park. He was so close to the man that he was able to say later that the man was not wearing a raincoat at that moment and that he had observed that there were a number of coloured pens or pencils in the top pocket of his jacket.

In defence of their being caught in the toilets the man told William Carroll that he was very sorry but, "I am a stranger here and it was raining heavy - we just came in here to get out of the rain." They left the toilets and Mr Carroll followed them some way along the main drive towards the main gate, noting that the woman was limping as if from an ill-fitting shoe. The couple were also seen by another Park policeman, Joseph Shone, by the Boy Scout Statue (which in 1955 was situated along the main drive about 200 yards from the main gate - *see photo on next page* - but has since been moved to another site), who was later able to give the police a good description of the couple which reinforced that of William Carroll. Both

The Boy Scout statue in Arrowe Park where the couple were seen by a Park Policeman

policemen were positive later that they had never seen Alice Barton in the park before, claiming that they would have noticed her because of her grotesque appearance. The probability was that it was the man who had prior knowledge of the park - they had passed other toilets and shelters on their way into the park and it seems unlikely that they would have found the quietest section of the park so quickly without one of them knowing the layout. The time was 12.45pm. The rain ceased to pour down at last.

Mrs Caroline Parry-Evans was a passenger on the lower deck of an outward bound bus as it proceeded around the Arrowe Park roundabout on schedule at 12.50pm. As she looked out of the grimy, rain-smeared window she noticed a dirty, bedraggled woman on the Landican side of the roundabout. Five minutes later Mrs Vera Blondfield also noted that a man and woman were at the Arrowe Park bus shelter. She took them to be mother and son, though the latter looked more superior.

The Heswall to Birkenhead No 71 bus pulled in by the bus shelter on time at 12.58pm. Now the rain had stopped visibility was good for James Clancy, the driver, and he could not help but notice the ill-kempt pair at the bus stop. Two other people boarded the bus as the driver checked in his rear mirror to see if he could pull out safely. The conductor, Sydney Roberts,

The Pillbox Murder

particularly noticed the woman because she was scruffy and that her left ankle was swollen and she was limping. The couple this time sat on the lower deck and when Mr Roberts came to collect the fares the man tendered fourpence. As there were no twopenny fares on that route, the conductor queried their destination. "To the Prenton railway bridge," the man replied. Two interesting points arise from this; firstly the use of the term 'Prenton' would require some local knowledge as that was the correct name for the bridge, and secondly it was not possible to see the railway bridge from Arrowe Park or any signpost marking the Prenton boundary thus indicating that the man knew the bridge was there. The fare for this stage had been raised from twopence to twopence halfpenny in 1951 - perhaps the man

---

MURDER AT BIRKENHEAD

With reference to the murder of Alice Barton at Birkenhead on or about 21st September, 1955, the Police desire to interview the following described man who may be able to assist them in their enquiries:-

35 To 40 years, 5'4" / 7", complexion fresh, hair dark and brushed back, dark eyebrows, full face, long nose, pointed chin; wearing dark suit, brown shoes or sandals, carrying old macintosh. Spoke of owning a coach which he used for conveying workmen between Margate and Ramsgate during the railway strike. Also stated he had been in hospital for 12 months, during which time his coach had been used by another person and when he got the coach back the seats had been slashed.

This man may be wandering the country or may have gone to sea.

Any person having information which may assist in tracing this man, please communicate with the Chief Constable, Birkenhead, telephone number Birkenhead 6262 or the nearest Police Station.

Central Police Office,
Birkenhead
23rd November, 1955

The Police issued this description of a man they would have liked to interview

had not travelled on that route for more than four years. Was he a Wirral man who had been away from the district for some time?

The man and the woman alighted at the bus stop at Kenmore Road on the Birkenhead side of Prenton bridge and as the bus pulled away the conductor watched as the strange couple walked back under the bridge in the direction of Woodchurch. By a curious coincidence, Kenneth Sparrow, the bus driver who had seen Alice Barton at Moreton Cross earlier that day, was driving the Route 77 bus returning to Moreton from Woodside past Prenton bridge at 1.05pm and as it passed under the bridge he again saw the same two persons walking on his right-hand side between the bridge and the footpath to Upton which ran across the fields towards the pillbox. Ten minutes later Mrs Fidella Baker was sitting on the nearside seat of a bus bound for Birkenhead when it passed the footpath. She saw a woman who she later identified from photographs as Alice Barton, either sitting or crouching in the undergrowth adjoining the path. She was under the impression that another person was nearby and it appeared to her as though the woman was taking advantage of the undergrowth for use as a toilet. Without doubt Mrs Baker was the last person to see Alice Barton alive - that is except for her killer.

The footpath, which was known locally as a 'lovers walk' still leads from beside Prenton bridge to Flat Lanes and on to Upton. At a distance of about 800 yards from Woodchurch Road on the right there is another railway bridge and the pillbox was approximately 25 yards beyond this and along the railway embankment (the concrete base of the pillbox is still there today). The pillbox was only visible from Woodchurch Road from the top deck of a bus or from a train travelling on the railway. This bridge and the pillbox were the only places of shelter in inclement weather for anyone who wished to keep their affairs private between Arrowe Park and the houses on the Birkenhead side of Prenton Bridge. It seems inconceivable that neither Alice Barton nor her killer had any pre-knowledge of this spot - after all they had deliberately asked for fares to Prenton bridge, alighted from the bus and walked back towards the footpath. To have come upon the pillbox by accident is to stretch the bounds of reason.

By the time that Alice Barton's body had been identified the police had

The SS Empress of France - *crew members were interviewed by the police*

published a description of the man they wanted to interview in the local papers and in the *Police Gazette (see page 21)*. Many police forces around the country replied to this plea for help in finding the killer but eventually all these enquiries resulted in dead-ends.

The editor of the *Daily Post and Echo* was not pleased to be asked again for help in view of the way that he felt his newspaper had been treated after the publication of Alice Barton's photograph. The picture of her was so horrible that other papers did not print it (*see page 10*). However, the partial identification of the murdered woman resulted directly from it being published in the *Liverpool Echo* - as the following morning's London papers named the woman as Alice Barton. However, the Birkenhead police withheld this information from the *Post & Echo* saying that the body was still unidentified. This resulted in a letter being sent to the Chief Constable from the Assistant Managing Director of the *Liverpool Daily Post & Echo*, Mr AG Jeans, who was disappointed with the lack of co-operation.

Detective Inspector Miller had more pressing things to worry about than newspaper editors. He had turned his attention to one particular aspect of the case; the fact that Alice Barton had been in the *St Winefred's* public house in Bootle at the time that the *S.S. Empress of France* docked in Liverpool. Twenty police officers led by Detective Inspector Miller (*see photograph on previous page*) were sent to interview every member of the 340 strong crew including the 80 members who were paid off on the 20 September. Cecil McLeavy, the barman from the *Arrowe Park Hotel,* was present at all these interviews but was unable to identify anyone of the crew as the man he had served on the day Alice Barton died.

A similar check was made on all personnel and civilian staff at the Royal Air Force camp at West Kirby. The movements of absentees and night-shift workers at Cammell Laird shipyard were checked and lists of local men with criminal records, especially for indecency and assault, were prepared. Both Birkenhead Corporation bus company and Crosville Bus Company staff, Park's employees and Council staff were all seen by police officers. Every one of their statements was checked and by the time the enquiry was finished over 100 ships which had been in the Mersey at the time of the murder had had every member of the crew checked out, over 1000 statements were on record and almost 40,000 people in total had had their movements checked on that day.

Great hopes were placed on forensic science in the 1950s to provide the police with positive information which could lead to a conviction and this case was no exception. Even the toilet door at Arrowe Park was carefully taken off and sent to the forensic laboratory for fingerprinting. But one piece of evidence which might have been of real help to the police enquiry was at the forensic laboratory for a whole week after the finding of the body. This was the copy of the *Daily Mirror* newspaper which was found in the pillbox and which was being carefully examined for fingerprints when other information that the paper contained could have been investigated immediately. On the Monday following the finding of Alice Barton's body the laboratory telephoned the police to inform them that they had obtained no forensic evidence from the newspaper. They had, however, noted the names of four horses which had been marked off in the racing section in the paper; *Loves Girdle* and *Problem Boy* both in the 2pm race; *River Belle* and *Le Can Can* in the 2.30; all at Brighton [interestingly the favourite in the 3.30pm race was Madge **Barton** - the surname of the murdered woman - but this horse had not been circled]. George Miller immediately started an investigation into this new piece of evidence. The Superintendent claimed in his final report that all the bookmakers and their runners on Merseyside had been interviewed and their records searched but it must be remembered that betting was illegal at that time and bets were taken by bookies runners in public houses, on building sites and on street corners to be passed clandestinely to the back rooms of terrace houses where the bookies sat with the racing papers and their radios; It was probable that the police did not receive the full co-operation of the betting community as they would be loathe to open up their operations to the prying eyes of the law.

How the man had obtained the newspaper was another question which does not seem in hindsight to have been satisfactorily answered. The *Daily Mirror* newspaper found in the pillbox was printed in London and forwarded to Liverpool for distribution to various parts of Lancashire and Cheshire. Over two hundred were delivered to houses

The racing page of the Daily Mirror, *found in the pill box, which had been marked off - see previous page*

in the Moreton area on that particular morning and the recipients were all traced and interviewed. The paper, however, bore no newsagents mark and might well have been purchased over the counter. Also, and this was something that the police appear not to have considered, it might have been picked up by the man on the buses or at one of the bus shelters, in Arrowe Park or in the *Arrowe Park Hotel*. In reality it might not have belonged to him at all and the horses underlined on the race page could have been marked by someone else. But we are missing one factor at this point - the part of the paper which had a section torn out and the possible clue that it contained - something which seems to have been overlooked while the newspaper was at the forensic laboratory and was not investigated until too late.

Had the request for the free apron been filled in and sent to the Unilever Company; had it been torn out and put in the pocket of the killer to apply later or had it just been thrown away? By the time the police were able to contact Unilever all the signed

Was this advert from the Daily Mail the vital clue that the police missed?
(see this page)

and addressed requests had been dispatched and no record had been kept of the recipients.

Detective-Superintendent Miller was nothing if not thorough, when it came to making lists of persons to be interviewed. Men who lived in lodging houses were catalogued, persons released from mental hospitals, persons visiting VD clinics, coach owners and drivers, men who were in any way similar to the description given by witnesses, but when it came to tracing all the men known to have associated with Alice Barton, as with any prostitute, the police were confronted with an insurmountable task. As is still the case today, not every man who has used a prostitute wishes to come forward and be identified!

Local thieves, prostitutes and anyone regularly known to frequent the landing stages were interrogated. Shops and public houses in the area were visited as were building sites where men had been 'rained off' on the morning of the murder. Two hundred photographs in all of local men with criminal records were obtained from the Criminal Record Office and an album of 'suspects' built up. All persons released from Walton Prison that year who were responsible for sexual and wounding offences of a similar nature were interviewed and the movements of all persons arrested after 21 September were checked together with any suicides in Merseyside after that date.

Even dry-cleaning establishments 'throughout the country' were checked for bloodstained clothing although there was only a small amount in the pillbox and the killer's clothes would have been unlikely to have been splattered with blood. Two unlucky police constables were dispatched to spend a week combing the Seaforth foreshore for Alice Barton's handbag. Every avenue was being explored to trace the killer.

None of these enquiries led in a positive direction and at the end of two weeks Detective-Superintendent Miller had a list of only eight suspects, one of whom inexplicably was George Kendrick as he was old and walked with a stick. By checking all their movements over the material time and confronting them with witnesses, such as Cecil McLeavy and William Carroll the Superintendent was forced to accept that none of the men on his list could have been responsible for the death of Alice Barton. Fourteen thousand homes had been visited, forty thousand people interviewed, nearly one thousand statements taken and hundreds of questionnaires completed and reports received. Detective-Superintendent Miller and his men were getting nowhere.

The inquest into the death of Alice Barton was held on 27 October 1955 at the Coroner's Court in Birkenhead. In attendance was Constable 217 Wood whose application for an attendance allowance of 2/6d ($12^{1}/_{2}$p) was authorised /by the Chief Constable (*see page 28*).

In June 1955, Miss Margaret Margerison, aged 27, an insurance clerk from

Port Sunlight, accompanied a friend named Doris Beddow on a coach holiday to the South Coast with a company named Stanley Spencer's Tours. She was employed as an insurance clerk and had saved all her hard-earned money for this holiday. The two friends were determined to enjoy themselves and the coach driver, who had knowledge of the area from previous trips, was most helpful. He paid particular attention to

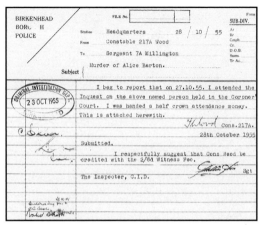

Constable Wood's attendance allowance application for the inquest of Alice Barton

Miss Margerison and within two days the relationship had blossomed into romance; at least in the eyes of Margaret Margerison. Before the holiday was over the driver, Edward William Clark, sometimes known as 'Ted' or 'Bill', had 'seduced her under promise of marriage', and Margaret returned to Wirral a happy young woman. What she did not know, however, was that Edward Clark was married, and had a criminal record with convictions for false pretences, larceny and embezzlement at towns and cities across the country.

Clark continued to visit Margaret in Port Sunlight between his supposed coach trips and was known to be in the area on 21 September, 1955. Detective Superintendent Miller became more and more interested in Clark and was soon delving into his past. The address listed on his driving licence was Bickershaw, near Wigan, and enquiries revealed that he still had a wife and two children residing at The Vicarage, Bickershaw. As a teenager in the Wigan area had he known Alice Barton? Another curious coincidence was that in 1942 Clark was resident at the Akbar Nautical Training School at Heswall where he had been sent as a juvenile offender. So Clark had some local knowledge. Clark had also disappeared the day after the murder and had not been seen again by Miss Margerison, her mother or anyone else in the area. Had the police at last got a 'prime suspect'?

The Pillbox Murder

On 5 June 1956, Clark's details were published in the *Police Gazette* which had countrywide distribution. It is difficult now to see why Detective Superintendent Miller pursued this lead so thoroughly as the man pictured in the *Police Gazette* bore little resemblance to the description given of the 'unkempt man' by witnesses, not least that Clark quite obviously did not have a pointed chin or a sharp nose. Perhaps it was a symptom of the desperation which had by then crept into the investigation. Eventually Clark was arrested in Newmarket and George Miller went there to interview him. Not satisfied with his story Miller brought Clark back to Birkenhead for an identification parade. Cecil McLeavy, the man Detective-Superintendent Miller used at all identifications, was in no doubt when he saw Clark at Birkenhead police station that this was not the man he had served in the *Arrowe Park Hotel*. Further interrogation by George Miller revealed that Clark could not have been near the scene of the murder on that fateful day. The Detective Superintendent was at another dead end.

Eventually George Miller went back to Scotland Yard; there was nothing more that he could do. But the case was still open and in 1961 further enquiries were made by Detective Inspector Jack Hastie of the Birkenhead CID as a result of a letter received following the publication of an article in the now defunct *Sunday Pictorial* newspaper. The newspaper was running a series of articles on unsolved murders and was offering a £2500 reward for information leading to the arrest of the perpetrators. The handwritten letter suggested that a local man employed as a bus driver was responsible - the writer had been present in the canteen of the Crosville Bus Company and had 'overheard a conversation' in which someone had boasted about the killing. The man was named in the letter and Jack Hastie interviewed the man in the offices of his solicitors, Percy Hughes and Roberts of Hamilton Square, Birkenhead. The accusation in the letter was found to be false - perhaps the writer had been motivated by malice. Once again what had started as a promising lead fizzled away to nothing.

Over forty years on the case is still open and the murderer of Alice Barton has never been found. We are left with a tantalising thought - perhaps the murderer is still alive. The only hope now of finding the killer may be a deathbed confession.

Chapter two

THE LISCARD GENTLEMAN
AND THE ACTRESS

The gentleman in question was Mr Edgar S Holland, of 'Stoneleigh', 11 Penkett Road, Wallasey and it is necessary at this point to fill in some details of his life preceding his untimely death in 1896 at the age of 49. Mr Holland was a successful businessman with offices at 45 Drury Buildings, Liverpool. He had investments in a number of mining companies, two of which he was managing director of, and was reputed to be worth a quarter of a million pounds - a very considerable sum in those days. He was a bachelor with a keen interest in the theatre and on one of his visits to the theatre in 1895 was overwhelmed by the beauty of a Miss Catherine Kempshall, also known as Mrs West. She was 'an actress known in Liverpool, London and other dramatic circles'. Miss Kempshall was always a very fashionably attired lady and was described as 'fascinating in appearance'. She was just thirty years of age when she was introduced to Edgar Holland.

The two became not only friends but, according to the actress, Mr Holland proposed marriage. At a 'breach of promise' trial in the London Courts early in 1896, Miss Kempshall claimed that Mr Holland had agreed to settle £10,000 upon her on their marriage. The famous QC, Sir Edward Clarke, appeared for Mr Holland but Miss Kempshall conducted her own case. The jury's verdict was that there was no case for the plaintiff although Mr Holland was required to pay the plaintiff £1000 and costs. Miss Kempshall was apparently not pleased with this outcome and charged across the court screaming, "You beast, you beast, pay me, pay me!" and had to be forcibly restrained by the court ushers.

This was not her only excess as she had only the day before the 'breach of promise' trial began been acquitted at the Old Bailey on the charge of 'discharging a loaded revolver' at Mr Holland's sister in Putney with intent

Penkett Road, Liscard pictured in the early part of this century

to murder. The Judge in his summing up had advised her, "Not to allow her supposed grievances to influence her temper in the future." She had told the police that she only intended to frighten Mr Holland's sister in order to bring her grievances to the public attention. On 23 December 1895 she had also been charged at the Mansion House Police Court, London, with assaulting a solicitor's clerk. According to the evidence she had been 'persistently annoying Mr Holland, his solicitors, and in fact, everyone engaged in the 'breach of promise' case, including members of Mr Holland's family.' On one visit to the solicitor's offices she had said that she would get the senior partner 'struck off.' She dealt Mr Boughton, the clerk, a violent blow with the back of her hand, screaming, "I will give you all more of that."

Catherine Kempshall eventually refused a further offer by Mr Holland to pay her £900 down and an allowance of £100 a year and she was bound over to keep the peace for six months and to find £50 surety, or go to gaol for two weeks.

This was not the end of the matter. A newspaper report on 31 October 1896 describes the events that followed her enraged loss of the 'breach of promise' case:-
'On Thursday afternoon the commercial activity of Water Street, Liverpool, was suddenly disturbed by the report that a well-known merchant had been attacked in his office, shot by a lady, and was at the point of death'.

The Liscard Gentleman and the Actress

Mr Holland and his solicitor, Mr JW Alsop, had gathered in his private office to meet Miss Kempshall in order to put an end to her harassment. It was a large oval table, Mr Holland sat at one end, Miss Kempshall at the other and Mr Alsop between them. Could he, he hoped, pour oil on the troubled waters?

They had talked for some time when suddenly Miss Kempshall rose to her feet, drew a revolver from her pocket and shot Mr Holland at point blank range. He staggered to his feet but the actress, far from being terrified at what she had done, proceeded to fire four more chambers of the gun. Mr Alsop leapt up and held the infuriated woman. The shots had been heard by Mr Holland's clerks who summoned the police. Two constables arrived quickly on the scene. One of them described the scene:-

'Mr Holland lay on the floor in a pool of blood. He was semiconscious. Mr Alsop was holding a lady of prepossessing appearance who seemed calm but had a determined attitude. She was glowering with fiendish delight at the prostrate body of Mr Holland.'

She must have been a very attractive woman for the constable to take in her appearance and expression while a man lay dying on the floor.

In a police report on the case it was noted that, "she exhibited the greatest nonchalance throughout the proceedings. She retained full mastery of herself and answered the questions put to her with perfect composure. She is a tall, good-looking lady, and wore a sealskin jacket and a considerable amount of jewellery. She is apparently about thirty years of age, of somewhat athletic build and exhibited a certain hauteur in her demeanour, which seemed to show that she understood everything about the occurrence and made no attempt to conceal its gravity."

In an interview in her cell she declared, "I shot at his legs. I did not mean to do more than frighten him. I did not mean to do him any serious injury."

Catherine Kempshall was tried for murder before Mr Justice Collins at Liverpool Assizes on 21 March 1897. She appeared in court sombrely but neatly dressed in black, with a short elegant cape, feathered boa and a flecked straw hat. She was tense and nervous throughout the trial. On one

The Liscard Gentleman and the Actress

occasion she 'furiously clenched her fist at someone in the court.'

Mr W Madden appeared for the defence and his clever speech was based on the premise that she was 'labouring under delusions and not responsible for her actions', a view subsequently supported by medical evidence and the tone of her letters to Mr Holland after the 'breach of promise' trial. He defined her state as that of 'persecution mania'. However, when Mr Madden stated this diagnosis she cried indignantly from the dock, "I am not mad, I am quite sane." The jury retired for only one and a half hours to return with a verdict of 'Guilty' but with a strong recommendation for mercy. Miss Kempshall was quite composed as the Judge donned his black cap and pronounced the words of the death sentence. His final words, "And may God have mercy on your soul," rang with sincerity.

By the end of March Miss Kempshall had lapsed into a state of abject misery, remaining silent for hours on end, brooding and gazing vacantly into space. She seemed to have given up any idea of life.

The execution had been fixed for 6 April but an appeal to the Home Secretary had been launched immediately for a reprieve. Eventually more than 15,000 signatures were obtained; some Liverpool bank clerks sent a special petition for the mercy of the Crown and even the Holland family signed their names in favour of a commutation of the sentence. An American woman of seventy years of age, living in Victoria Square, Liverpool, trudged the streets of the city from office to office and collected 700 signatures, mainly from women. As she said, "In America, I guess, any woman would have shot a man in such circumstances."

Mr Quilliam, who had been Miss Kempshall's solicitor from the beginning of the case, co-ordinated the collection of signatures and forwarded petitions to the Home Secretary, who, on 5 April, one day before her proposed execution, wrote to Mr Quilliam that he had advised Her Majesty to 'respite the capital sentence with a view to the immediate removal of the prisoner to the Broadmoor Criminal Lunatic Asylum' and her transfer was completed that day. Catherine Kempshall spent the next fifty-six years in Broadmoor where she died aged 88 in 1953.

Chapter three

AN OLD SEACOMBE SMUGGLER?

Mrs Stallybrass was in her early sixties in 1932 when she recalled an incident which occurred when, as a child, she lived with her parents at St Paul's Vicarage, then in Wheatland Lane, occupied from 1878 till 1883 by Canon Weatherhead:-

"One of my sisters, then less than two years old, was frightened one night after being put to bed, and kept saying, "Man, man." She was finally soothed and went back to sleep. During that same night three people in the house heard somebody go downstairs from the top floor to the cellar kitchen, each taking it to be an inmate of the house. None of them remembered hearing any return steps, and in the morning each member of the household denied having been up at all during the night. The doors were found bolted on the inside as usual, and the windows all latched. As the whole family was to go away that day and the house was to be shut up for some weeks, it was feared somebody might be in hiding awaiting a chance to rifle the place. A thorough search was made, but with no result, and the whole thing remained a mystery.

Some years later, after we had left the house, in the course of some repairs to the flags of the kitchen floor, under one flag which had always been loose, there was discovered the entrance to an underground passage of some length. It was filled in at once, and never fully explored, but it was always my father's belief that it was an old smugglers' passage leading to the shore, and that my sister had actually been frightened by a strange man, an old smuggler perhaps, who made his way out by the old passage."

Was this one of the subterranean smugglers' passages known to have been under Demesne Street in Wallasey? Perhaps some of those passages are still there; perhaps the bones of the old smuggler of Mrs Stallybrass' story are still raising ghosts on moonlit nights in the area.

Chapter four

A SCANDALOUS AFFAIR IN LISCARD

On Monday evening 16 April 1917, the brutal double murder of a mother and child was committed in a house in Central Park Avenue, Liscard. The victims were Margaret Alderson Hodgson, 37, and her daughter, also Margaret, who was just four years old some days before the murders.

Mrs Eleanor Law, who lived next door, was a pleasant, neighbourly woman who befriended Mrs Hodgson on her arrival in the town and they saw each other most days. On the day of the murders she had not seen Mrs Hodgson or anyone in the house but the baby had been crying continuously for hours. Mrs Hodgson was, in Mrs Law's view, a good mother, and it was most unusual for the baby to be left to cry like that. Shortly before 6pm, her curiosity aroused by the fact that she had not seen her neighbour moving about the house as usual, she crept up to the front door of the house. The door was open, she knocked and listened; there was no reply. Pushing open the door she ventured inside the vestibule and along the hall. She could still hear the baby crying upstairs but went to look in the front room first. Nothing struck her as odd except for an open portmanteau which was usually locked. Nothing in the back room. There was no-one in the kitchen either. Finally she pushed open the back kitchen door to see the lower part of a woman's body lying on the floor. She was frightened by the fleeting glimpse she had seen and ran back into the street straight into a passer-by, who was making his way to the shops for some cigarettes. She stammered out the story to the man who accompanied her back to the scullery and the scene of carnage. As she had feared, there was something tragically wrong. On the floor of the back kitchen close to the back door were the bodies of the mother and child. Their heads had been battered in with a bloodstained hatchet, which was found lying between the bodies. The child had received a single vicious blow to the side of the head which had evidently killed her instantly. In the case of the mother she had received multiple injuries to the head such that her brain protruded from the skull on the right-hand side.

A Scandalous Affair in Liscard

William Wells, the passer-by dragged into this gruesome event, went upstairs and removed the baby from its cot. The baby was handed over to Hannah Lancaster who lived at 22 Central Park Avenue and she took the baby home with her. Mr Wells went off to the police station and then on to his home in Royston Avenue to try to recover from what he had seen.

Just after 6.30pm Detective Inspector Robert Pearson arrived at the house. He examined the scullery carefully. There was no sign of a struggle and no sign of forced entry. A pool of blood stained the floor beside the gas stove at one end of the room and there was another pool of blood at the opposite end near the yard door. Splashes of blood speckled one of the walls and cupboards. There was blood on the gas stove and on some crockery hanging from a shelf. Under the scullery window was a draining board and on this was a pastry board on which was a partly-cut loaf as if someone had started to cut a slice of bread. Mrs Hodgson's blood-spattered spectacles were also on the pastry board and some bloodstained crockery on the drainer. On the floor was a breadknife. Had she been facing the window cutting the loaf when she was struck from behind on her right-hand side? This would have caused her to drop the breadknife to her right as she fell to the left where her body was found. The back door was unlocked but would only open a matter of inches as the child's body was lying close to it indicating that the perpetrator had left by the front door. On the kitchen table was her empty purse and an empty money-box. One of the dressing table drawers in the front bedroom was open and several articles of jewellery had been disturbed. The portmanteau was also unlocked and open. He looked at the portmanteau more closely. There was a bag inside containing some electroplated silver items but they were worth little. Other items including a silver-plated toast rack, a sugar bowl and biscuit barrel, and a silver clock were scattered across the floor. Robbery was the first motive that came to mind for the Inspector. Perhaps the thief or thieves had been disturbed and left the bag behind in their hurry to escape their terrible crime. But would a thief bring a hatchet on a simple burglary? Both mother and child had their hair in curlers. The loaf of bread was cut halfway through on the kitchen table as though they had been disturbed in the act of making a meal and as they were still dressed in nightclothes it was evident that they had been killed soon after they had risen from their beds and possibly while making breakfast. Post-mortem examination later revealed that neither Mrs Hodgson or the child had eaten that morning; the beds were unmade and the baby in the cot upstairs had not been attended to. The time of death appeared to be between 8.30am and 9am. An ambulance was sent for and the bodies removed to Seacombe Ferry mortuary.

And what of Mr Hodgson? William Thomas Hodgson was a buyer, aged 34, in the employ of Robb Brothers, Grange Road, Birkenhead. He had worked for them since April, 1916 but his wife had been living in Huddersfield and had not joined him until August. Up to this time Hodgson had lived in the residential part of Robb Brothers, known as Sutton House. On the arrival of his wife they rented the house in Central Park Avenue at 26 pounds per year. His salary was then 55 shillings (£2.75) per week with a commission of ten shillings (50 pence) per week. The couple had married on 14 September 1910 at Harpurhey, Manchester, when he was 28 and she was 30. They had two children, Margaret four and Cyril 12 months old.

He was in the habit of leaving for work at about 8.30am, lunching at work or in a nearby cafe, and returning home in the evening. On the day of the murders, Mrs Law, who was a very observant woman, had heard footsteps in the yard of the Hodgson's house at around 8.30am and the voice of a child saying, "Don't do that." At 8.40am she was sure that she heard the

Robb Brothers Store, Grange Road, Birkenhead, where Wm Hodgson worked

front door bang as if Mr Hodgson was going to work. He was seen by other members of staff at Robb Brothers at 9.25am and he was present at the shop, except for a half-hour lunch, until he left work in the evening. He did not record his arrival in the register in the usual way and something strange also happened about midday. Miss Florence Sparke, an employee in the silk department, was accosted by a Mrs Llewellyn in the shop. She was looking for Hodgson but Miss Sparke could not find him as he was out at lunch. On his return Florence told him of Mrs Llewellyn's visit and his comment was, "If she calls again tell her to mind her own business." He was, in her words, "very agitated" by the visit. On his arrival home he was met by Chief Inspector Morris. "What's wrong?" asked Hodgson. "Something is seriously wrong," said the Inspector as he led Hodgson into the front room. On seeing the open portmanteau, Hodgson pointed at it and said, "That's wrong, look at that." Was Hodgson merely indicating the open chest or was he trying to imply that a burglary had taken place to put the police off the scent, thought the Inspector. Chief Inspector Morris made no mention of what had befallen Mrs Hodgson and the child, and took Hodgson down to the police station without showing him the scullery. At the police station Hodgson made a statement as to his whereabouts throughout the day and then was taken back to the house. In the meantime the bodies had been removed to Seacombe Ferry mortuary and the hatchet placed for safe keeping on the mantelpiece in the kitchen. When Hodgson was shown into the kitchen he immediately noticed the hatchet and said, "That hatchet is not mine!" although he had still not been told about his wife and daughter, or indeed the way in which they had been killed. Returning to the police station his clothing was taken from him, including a topcoat with spots of blood on it. Chief Inspector Morris was certain that he had the murderer; Hodgson's story was unsubstantiated and his answers to the Inspector's questions most unsatisfactory. When Hodgson was eventually told of the fate of his wife and daughter he buried his head in his hands and sobbed. Was this a show of genuine feelings for the cruel fate that had taken away his family? Was it remorse? Or was it just play-acting? Chief Inspector Morris favoured the latter and charged Hodgson with the murder of his wife and child.

Where did the peculiar visit of Mrs Llewellyn to his place of work fit into the story? About Easter, 1916, while his wife was still living in Huddersfield, Hodgson went to Evans' Cafe, next door to Robb Brothers, and was introduced by a friend to a young lady named Helen Llewellyn who was a waitress at the cafe. He met her again that same evening. They met frequently after that, two or three times a week, and he was taken to her home at 14 Mellor Road, Prenton on several occasions. Their friendship became more intimate as the year went by and in the March of 1917 the young woman's mother became suspicious that her daughter was pregnant. She took her to a medical specialist who confirmed the fact. On 21 March Mrs Llewellyn called at Robb Brothers to see Hodgson and about 6.30 that evening he called at the Llewellyn house where he was informed of the girl's condition. He said that he would 'stand by her', but that he could do nothing until after Easter.

In a letter to Miss Llewellyn dated 1 April Hodgson wrote, "If you have the patience to wait until after Easter we will make some arrangements, so don't worry, it will be all right. We will meet soon and I think we shall both be satisfied, and your mother too." The Easter holiday period was 6 April to 9 April and over that weekend the Hodgsons entertained guests; Mrs Hodgson's sister and her husband. There would be no escape for William Hodgson that weekend and the pressure must have been mounting. Not only were his in-laws in the house but his wife had hired a young serving girl to help at the house from 8.30am to 8.30pm every day from the week before to the end of the week after Easter.

The case was heard at Chester Assizes before Mr Justice Avery. Mr Ellis Griffiths, KC MP appeared for the Crown and Mr Lindon Riley for the defence. The prosecution's case revolved about Hodgson's inability to produce a substantiated alibi for the period between 8.30am and 9.25am; the affair with Miss Llewellyn as motive; and the blood on his clothes. In opening the case for the prosecution Mr Ellis pointed out that Hodgson had quarrelled with his wife on occasions in the past and at the time of the murders they were occupying separate bedrooms. Mrs Hodgson was sleeping with the girl in the front bedroom and Mr Hodgson, with the boy occupying a cot, in the back room. Had an argument arisen that morning which had culminated in the brutal death of Mrs Hodgson? Had the child been present in the kitchen when the attack took place or had she come into the kitchen in response to her mother's cries? Perhaps the child had thought she could protect her mother only to be felled with one fatal blow.

Mr Ellis went on to describe the condition of the house. The doors and windows had been examined and there was no sign of forced entry. In the kitchen there were no signs of disorder or of a struggle. On the kitchen table was an empty purse and an empty money box. The portmanteau in the front sitting-room had been open and some articles from it strewn about the floor and a sideboard drawer was pulled out. Was the motive for this heinous crime really robbery and was it the work of a burglar? The prosecution held the view that this had all been done deliberately by Hodgson to lead suspicion away from himself.

William Hodgson's account of his activities on that fateful morning indicated that he was in the habit of rising first and making a cup of tea,. This he had taken to his wife in bed and later she had come down to make the breakfast for them. He had left the house at about 8.30am as his wife was getting the breakfast ready. "I had arranged, before I went to work, that my wife should go to the pictures that evening and I would stay in with the boy," he stated. "As far as I could see everything was as normal that morning."

Mrs Eliza Godfrey, who lived opposite the Hodgson's house in Central Park Avenue stated that on the morning in question she had seen William Hodgson leave the house and as he walked down the street she had noticed that he has stopped and stooped down twice as if brushing something off his trousers. Elsie Todd, the young 12 year old maid that Mrs Hodgson had employed over the Easter period added her knowledge of the domestic scene. She remembered that Mrs Hodgson always got up to prepare her husband's breakfast which he generally had by himself in the kitchen. As to the matter of the hatchet, she had never seen the bloodstained hatchet before but she had seen Mrs Hodgson use another hatchet which was kept in the scullery. William Smith, of Moston, Manchester, did nothing to help his son-in-law's case when he remarked from the witness box that Hodgson had 'an ungovernable temper, especially when he was under the influence of drink.' Thomas Davies, a salesman at Robb Brothers, attested that on the evening of 16 April he had asked Hodgson if he would stop to 'have a glass' before he went home but Hodgson had demurred on the grounds that he had to go straight home as his wife was going to the pictures. William Wilson, a warehouseman at Robbs, accompanied Hodgson home that evening and they stopped off at the *Charing Cross Hotel* for a drink; Wilson noticed nothing unusual about his companion's behaviour. Florence Sparke, who worked in the same department as Hodgson, remembered him telling her that he had cut himself shaving but she could not remember seeing a cut on his face.

Dr Bernard Spilsbury, the country's leading forensic expert at that time (he had given evidence at the Dr Crippen murder - *see chapter 10*), was called for his opinion about the blood stains. He told the court that although he was sure that the blood was that of the victims because of the distribution on the clothing he had been unable to complete serum tests due to the lack of material. He was certain that the blood stains were not as a result of a nose bleed or a shaving cut as Hodgson had claimed and he was sure that the blood on the garments was not as old as Hodgson had claimed. Tests on the hatchet revealed that the bloodstains were undoubtedly human blood. A tool box which was found in the lumber room of the house was produced in court. The murder weapon was shown to fit into this tool box but the significance of this piece of evidence had to be somewhat dubious.

William Hodgson was extremely self-possessed as he walked across the court to the witness box. He took the oath in a clear, firm voice. When questioned about his relationship with Helen Llewellyn his answers were almost arrogant. "How soon after you had met her did any impropriety take place between you and her?" - "A few days later," was his reply. "I never loved her and I had wearied of her by Christmas," he said in response to enquiries about his feelings for the shamed girl. "Do you acknowledge that you are the father of this child?" "No." - "What explanation do you have of the letters to this girl telling her not to worry and that she would be with you soon?" - "That was a mutual arrangement between ourselves for the purposes of misleading her mother. We didn't want Mrs Llewellyn to know that I was a married man." Miss Llewellyn had claimed that she did not know he was a married man until late the previous month. If Hodgson could admit to guile and deceit in his relationship with Helen Llewellyn was he not employing the same deceit in the face of a jury of his peers?

Mr Ellis KC, in his final speech for the prosecution, stressed the fact that Hodgson had no substantiated alibi for the period between 8am and 9am on the day of the murders, that by his own admission in court he had deceived not only Helen Llewellyn and her mother but also his wife with his Lothario-like conduct, that he had repudiated in court the paternity of the child and that there was clear motive for this ghastly crime. As to his conduct at work that day it had been described as not being unusual, but a man who was able to give his evidence as coolly as he did was a man of strong nerve. When Hodgson had arrived home that evening there had been an ambulance outside his house; he had not even questioned its presence. Would not a normal man have asked about the health and safety of his family instead of walking straight into the front room to examine the portmanteau? For the defence Mr Lindon Riley pressed the theory that the murders were done by a burglar and that Hodgson's demeanour at work indicated a lack of guilt.

The Judge took two hours to sum up the evidence. "The burden of proof," he said, "was on the prosecution to satisfy the jury that the prisoner in the dock was guilty beyond reasonable doubt. If the jury thought that the evidence was consistent with the view that the murders were committed by some person who entered the house after Hodgson had left, then he was entitled to be acquitted." He reiterated the point that when Hodgson arrived back at the house and was asked to go to the police station, "Could the jury imagine any man in such a position not asking what had happened to his wife and child. If a thief committed the murders and was disturbed while rifling through the house, why should he not have taken his ill-gotten gains [the items from the portmanteau] with him when he knew that he had silenced the only two people who could identify him?"

The jury retired for only 11 minutes and as they filed back into their places, Hodgson stood with downcast eyes and without any show of emotion heard the verdict of 'Guilty'. He remained impassive as the Judge pronounced sentence and afterwards walked jauntily without assistance out of the dock and down the steps to the his cell.

Chapter five

THE WALLASEY CABINET MAKER AND THE YOUNG LADY

The courtroom at Liverpool Assizes on Monday 6 February 1928 was crowded and many of those who attended the trial of George Graham, a 54 year old cabinet maker, were from the Borough of Wallasey. More than a hundred people clamoured for admittance to the cramped courtroom but many were unable to gain entry. The majority were women, for the case involved the death of a 15 year old girl, Kathleen Lavinia (Vinnie) Cowburn, her death having caused a sensation in the tightknit community in which she lived. There was little sympathy for the man who stood accused of her murder as the case involved the classic constituents of an older man associated with a young girl, debauchery, abortion, drugs; everything that was guaranteed to keep the town in gossip for months to come.

Mr Justice Rigby Swift was the presiding judge, Mr Wingate Saul KC and Mr Noel Goldie appeared for the prosecution, and Mr Hemmerde KC and Mr R C Essenhigh acted for Graham who sat motionless listening attentively to all the evidence throughout his trial.

Mr Wingate Saul detailed the case for the prosecution. The allegation was that George Graham and Vinnie Cowburn had agreed upon a suicide pact. It was the law of the country that if two people agreed to commit suicide together and one survived, the survivor was guilty of murder. His intention was to show that this was the case.

George Graham, a thin, balding man, carried on his business as a furniture dealer and cabinet maker in a workshop in Park Street, Wallasey. He was well respected and had been in business in the area for over 20 years. He had known the girl's family for some years, having done some small jobs for them, and Vinnie, who was good with her hands, was in the habit of visiting his workshop to help him to make small pieces such as boxes. Vinnie lived at 61 Belgrave Street and her full time occupation was as a probationer telegraphist at Liverpool's Head Post Office. She was bright and pretty, a cheerful young lady who was popular with her workmates at the Post Office. In her spare time she was a member of the Girl Guides.

In the early part of November 1927 her mother noticed something wrong with the girl and on 11 November she took Vinnie to one side to have a quiet word with her. On this occasion Vinnie kept her own counsel and when her mother again questioned her three days later, on the morning of the tragedy, before she left for work, Vinnie still felt unable to confide in her mother that she was expecting a baby. Before she went to Liverpool Vinnie called at the workshop to see George Graham; Graham was not at his place of business; she would have to talk to him when she came home from work.

Vinnie Cowburn left work that evening at 7pm in the company of two friends and walked with them as far as Whitechapel where they watched her board a tram for the Pierhead. From there she would get a ferry boat to Wallasey. Nothing more was seen of Vinnie until her mother found her on the point of death, on a bench in Graham's workshop over an hour later. George Graham's workshop was situated in Park Street and backed onto the houses in Belgrave Street. The workshop was a large shed which housed

Park Street, Liscard, the site of Graham's workshop

three benches, a gas stove, and above one of the benches was a gas bracket which was connected to a gas ring on the bench. The key to the workshop, when not in Graham's possession, was left in an outhouse nearby.

On the day of the tragedy George Graham arrived for work at about 8.30am from his home in Seaview Road just minutes after Vinnie Cowburn had called to see him. He went home for lunch and returned to the workshop until, at five o'clock, he decided to close up. He left the shop with one of his employees, a french polisher named Alan Billington, and just before they left Billington asked his employer if he should put out the fire which was in an enclosed pipe stove. "No it's not necessary, it will be all right." As they closed the door Billington noticed that George Graham did not put the key in the outhouse as usual. Was it Graham's intention to come back that evening? Did he want to keep the place warm in the knowledge that he would be meeting Vinnie later? Curiously, at about 6.45pm, after his tea at home, he announced that he was going back to the shop to put the fire out. It was a rare occurrence for him to go out in the evening, owing to his wife's ill health - in the previous six months he had only gone out once in the evening. On this particular evening his son would have to stay home and look after his mother instead of his planned trip to the cinema.

At about 8.30pm Mrs Cowburn was in the kitchen of her house when she was startled to hear a voice outside the kitchen door, saying, "Let me in." "Who is it?" she enquired. "Mr Graham," was the reply. When she opened the door, George Graham stood trembling on the doorstep. "I've found Vinnie on the bench," he said and before Mrs Cowburn could ask any more questions, he turned round and started off in the direction of the workshop. Mrs Cowburn followed him into the shop, which was in darkness, and there she was horrified to find her daughter lying on one of the benches. There was a strong smell of gas. She needed help and knowing that her son was in the Liscard Concert Hall in Manor Road she rushed round there to get him. He came and carried the girl from the shop to their home, from which she was taken by ambulance to the hospital. Meanwhile George Graham had gone to summon the police and arrived back at Belgrave Street in time to see the ambulance depart. He was not seen again until 11.30 that evening when he was found at home by his son. His clothing was wet and

The Wallasey Cabinet Maker and the Young Lady

he sat in a chair moaning and holding his head in his hands. His son could get no sense out of him so he went to the police station to let them know that his father had returned - they could stop searching for him. Graham was then taken to the police station where the Chief Constable, Mr Barry, was waiting to question him.

In a statement made that evening Graham said, "I may as well tell you. We were going to take gas, both of us. She was frightened to go home. We both agreed to do it. She drove me to it. In my right senses I would not have dreamed of it. I have been worried in the shop. My wife has been ill. It has preyed on my mind." Who was he referring to when he said, "She drove me to it?" Was it his wife? Undoubtedly not. If it was Vinnie Cowburn, she must have had an overpowering effect on him for him to agree to a suicide pact. Was it his suggestion to commit suicide together? Had he good reason to take his own life? The Chief Constable, Chief Inspector Ormerod and a Dr Martlew commenced an inspection of the workshop and found a gas ring on the bench and two sacks, one wrapped up like a pillow and the other with the gas tube leading into it. In the stove were found some pills and capsules, and some partly burnt papers. Lying around they found the girl's handbag, hat, a pair of gloves and a key. By the next day George Graham had had time to think; he retracted his statement. "I was not right when I said that. It was not right."

Six days later an undated note was found in the girl's mackintosh pocket. It was in George Graham's handwriting. It read:
"I have received your letter. Just happened to be in or someone would have opened it. You should send addressed G Graham, cabinet-maker, 34 Park Street. Enclosed is two shillings. Send on some next week. Glad you are enjoying yourself. With love, G G."

The note must have been sent some weeks prior to her death - Vinnie had been away with the Girl Guides on the August Bank Holiday but was it not strange for a young girl to keep a note like that in her pocket for so long after. Perhaps Vinnie's feelings for George Graham ran deeper than as a father figure. And why was Graham sending her money? Was it just as a friend or was there a more intimate connection?

The Wallasey Cabinet Maker and the Young Lady

Post-mortem examination revealed that Vinnie Cowburn had died from carbon-monoxide poisoning. She was also six to eight weeks pregnant. Her mother's suspicions were confirmed. But who was the father? Was it George Graham or was it another man. Or was Graham merely acting as father confessor to the young girl? Who had provided the pills and capsules that were intended to help her to abort the baby? Her workmates had seen her taking medicines and pills for some weeks before she died. Had George Graham been supplying her with the means to end the unborn child's life? When questioned about the pills Graham admitted that he had brought them over from Liverpool. He further admitted that he had met the pretty young telegraphist on that fateful night. In his initial statement - later retracted - he had said that he let them into the workshop with a Yale key. Was this the key that Alan Billington had seen him put in his pocket earlier? Ernest Croston, an apprentice at the workshop, was asked by Mr Justice Swift if Vinnie Cowburn knew where the key was kept. "Yes," he replied. "Did you at any time see any trace of familiarity between Graham and the girl?" "No, sir." William Cowburn, the girl's father, also admitted that he had never seen any hint of George Graham being improperly familiar with his daughter. He had never had any reason to complain of Graham's conduct towards Vinnie.

For the defence, George Graham was the only witness to be called. His answers to all the questions put to him were concise and clear, delivered in a calm and rational manner. He denied any familiarity with Vinnie Cowburn and insisted that he had only been trying to help her in her difficulties. He did not know who was the father of the child - Vinnie had not told him and he had not pressed the subject. They had met on several occasions in the weeks before her death to talk about her predicament. "She begged me to buy the pills and medicines for her," he said under cross-examination. "Yes, I did advise her and yes, I did get the tablets for her," he admitted. Ironically the tablets were useless, they were purely laxatives. "I went down to the ferry to meet her that night and we walked back to the Liscard Road, Martins Lane junction together talking about what she should do about telling her mother. We parted company there and I thought Vinnie was going home."

The Wallasey Cabinet Maker and the Young Lady

Mr Hemmerde in his final speech to the jury was striking and eloquent. He pointed out the inconsistencies in the testimony that the jury had heard. "Would Mr Graham have thrown the pills and capsules on the fire if he had made an arrangement to die? If he had would he not have made sure that they were destroyed in the fire? He has said on oath that he had advised the girl to throw away the pills and to tell her mother about her condition. Which is likely, that the girl wanted to destroy these wretched medicines, or that the man, having agreed to die with her, wanted to destroy them? It has been suggested that any man who took upon himself the responsibility of getting medicine of that sort was doing it because he was the guilty person. This was not proved."

" She has the medicines with her," said Mr Hemmerde, "she knows where the key is kept. She goes into the workshop and finds the small stove burning. She takes a bill head - any paper lying about - anything to make a blaze, and throws them on the fire...........I suggest that the state in which these were found seems that it was her act and not his, and that he was never there at all. Whether she went in with the intention of using the gas ring or whether it flashed upon her that here was a way out, we shall never know. When you look at what was actually found there, the position of the sack, and, in fact, everything found there suggests that one person only took steps to end life, and not two."

"Is it not likely that Graham, discovering the tragedy in his workshop - finding the girl lying there like a broken blossom - should wander off into the night, absolutely crushed not only by what he had seen, but in fear because he had lent himself to doing what was illegal?"

Carefully and deliberately Mr Hemmende progressed through each piece of prosecution testimony and brought to each an element of doubt. He concluded his speech with these words, "Here is a man charged with a grave offence, but I suggest that everything in this case is against the theory of a suicide pact. If you are forced to the conclusion that there is a pact, by the evidence, then it is your duty to return a verdict of 'murder', but the man before you is entitled to every possible reasonable doubt, which you may have in considering this case. The responsibility is yours. To dwell on the horrors of the case, when a man's life hangs on your decision, is not safe. I leave my client entirely in your hands."

In his summing up Mr Justice Swift pointed out that some of the features of this case might offend against some people's sense of morality but that was not what the prisoner at the bar was being tried for. " If the statement made initially by Graham is correct," continued the judge, "then there is clear evidence that the girl met her death in consequence of an arrangement made with Graham, and that he was a party to her dying. That being so, then he is guilty of murder. Except for that statement there is no evidence of a suicide pact, and there is no allegation that murder was committed in any way."

After an absence of 40 minutes the jury, which consisted of ten men and two women, returned with a verdict of 'Not Guilty'. "Is my client discharged, my lord?" enquired Mr Hemmerde. "Yes, he may go," replied Mr Justice Swift. George Graham, who had betrayed no emotion throughout the trial, calmly picked up his hat and coat and left the dock. A large crowd of people waited outside the court to learn the result but failed to notice the lonely figure of George Graham walking calmly away in the direction of the ferry.

An interesting postscript to this case involves the key to the workshop. According to Alan Billington the key was not left in the outhouse. How then did Vinnie Cowburn gain access to the shop? Did she have a spare key or did Graham let her in? Furthermore, what was Graham really doing in the period between the time he alleged that he left Vinnie at the corner of Martins Lane around 7.30pm and the time he found her in his workshop? A whole hour had elapsed and the distance between the corner of Martins Lane and the workshop is no more than a few hundred yards. But there was one final question that would keep the tongues of Wallasey wagging for some time after the trial; was George Graham the father of Vinnie Cowburn's child? George Graham returned home to his ailing wife and must have survived the gossip because he was still living in the same house in Seaview Road fourteen years after the event.

Chapter six

AN ILLEGAL ABORTION IN LISCARD?

Jessie Moran was something of an enigma. She was a single woman but at the time of her death in May 1906 she was living at 8 Massey Park, Liscard under the name of Mrs Harper. She was forty years old and had two children, aged seven and eleven years, living with her. Both children were illegitimate. But the circumstances of her death indicated that there was a man in her life although her neighbours were unaware of her having male visitors or indeed having any relationships with men at all. Her sister, Mrs Frances Pierce, the wife of a joiner, of 53 Rossett Street, off Rocky Lane, Liverpool, went to visit her house on 26 April to find that her sister was ill in bed and stayed with her until Jessie's death on 18 May. Jessie Moran must have suffered severe pain before her death - at one point in that

Massey Park, Liscard, pictured in 1906

period Mrs Pierce called in a Dr Johnson and was present while he operated on her sister. The reason for the operation - Jessie Moran had had an abortion which had gone horribly wrong.

Dr Johnson confirmed Mrs Pierce's story. He stated that he had been called to the house on 1 May and found, after an examination, that she had had a miscarriage and peritonitis had set in. He performed an operation to extract a quantity of pus on that day. On 22 May he assisted a Dr Napier in making a post-mortem examination. The cause of death was septic peritonitis following abortion. In his opinion the abortion might have been caused criminally, or it might have been due to very great carelessness, which he thought was doubtful.

Detective Inspector Ennion was called to the house in Massey Park on the death of Jessie Moran and made a thorough search of the house in company with Mrs Pierce. In a dressing table drawer upstairs he found a letter and a card which interested him. Both the letter and the card were postmarked Liverpool and the letter was dated 21 February 1906. From the contents of the letter Detective Inspector Ennion and Detective Constable Pierpoint of the Liverpool City Police went to No 7, Breck Grove, off Queens Road, Everton, the residence of Sarah Jane Martin. Mrs Martin's answers to the Inspector's question were contradictory. "Yes," she said, "she had known Mrs Harper about three years ago but she had not communicated with her since."

Later she admitted that she had received a letter from Mrs Harper earlier that year which she had burned. When Detective-Inspector Ennion showed her the letter and the card she said that they were in her handwriting but the Inspector was a shrewd man - he got her to sign a statement at the end of the interview. Her writing was nothing like that of the letter or card.

Elizabeth Blebbin, a widow, of Southgate Road, Liverpool, was also interviewed by the police. She stated that from the end of February 1906 she had lodged with Sarah Martin at 7 Breck Grove. She admitted that the handwriting on the card and the letter belonged to her, but that she wrote them at the request of Sarah Martin and to her dictation. When the two women first met Sarah was single but in early March 1906 she married a Mr Martin who then disappeared from the scene. In late March or early April she and Mrs Martin went over to Liscard to see her son, but after the visit to her son Mrs Martin proposed that they also visit Mrs Harper. However, Mrs Blebbin's recollection of the conversation revealed nothing; it had revolved around 'women's talk'. No mention was made on that visit of medical assistance although Mrs Blebbin had been told previously by Sarah Martin that she had been a nurse.

It was established later that Sarah Martin had seen Mrs Harper on three further occasions both at Massey Park in Liscard and in Liverpool. According to Sarah Martin she had received requests from the deceased to supply her with medicines for an abortion but although she had examined her she had not acceded to the request for drugs.

In view of the contradictory evidence the magistrates, led by Mr Joynson, decided that they could not commit the case for trial on a charge of murder and that Sarah Jane Martin would remain in custody on a Coroner's warrant until a decision could be made. There our trail ends and there is no further reference to Mrs Martin or this alleged illegal abortion.

Chapter seven

DRAMATIC EVENTS IN LEASOWE - BUNGALOW TOWN

O n a moonless Monday evening in 1927 William Ingham quietly and carefully began to make some grim preparations in the rented bungalow in which he lived with his two illegitimate children, Barry, aged three,

"Fellowship House", Moreton, in the background with some of the 'bungalows'

and Dennis who was nearly two. The bungalow, called 'The Nook', was a small, wooden building in a field near 'Fellowship House', off Pasture Lane in Moreton.

Ingham himself was 53 years old and had been separated from his wife for some years but the children were the product of a liaison with a woman named Sarah Rickard. His fine physique and handsome appearance gave an impression that he was years younger than his actual age. He was an enthusiastic tennis player and the secretary of the Fellowship Sports Club.

Dramatic Events in Leasowe

People who knew this popular figure in Moreton, described him as refined and well-educated. He had qualified as a chartered accountant and until three years before had been employed in that capacity by a Liverpool firm of accountants. At that time he had met Sarah Rickard, fallen in love with her, and from that point in his life he had lost all interest in work. All he wanted was to be with her. But this was the twenties, the years of the Depression. He was soon dismissed from his job and was unable to find any other work. His wife, also Sarah, had left him at the start of the affair and gone to live in Beeston, Nottinghamshire. She had taken out divorce proceedings against him the previous year and had not seen him for two years but they had corresponded and she had sent him £25 recently because she knew that he was short of money. He had continued to live in the marital home and Sarah Rickard came to live with him. Sarah was a dark-haired, attractive young woman and they had two beautiful children whom he adored. But his life was becoming more and more financially insecure. Lack of money brought with it disagreements between the lovers and Sarah Rickard had begun to think about moving back to live in Liverpool.

The previous morning he had taken the children to the railway station to watch the trains but he did not have enough money to buy them sweets. He was depressed. On his return to the house he was in a foul mood and soon after the landlady arrived demanding the rent arrears of ten guineas (£10.50). He tried to mollify her by telling her that he would give her the rent by the end of the week but the landlady pointed out to him that if the rent was not forthcoming she would have to take proceedings against him; a course of action she did not care to take. "I would prefer it if you would go quietly," she told him.

After dinner Sarah and William began to quarrel and as he began to threaten her with physical violence Sarah fled out of the back door. She returned later to find the children being given their tea. Afterwards she undressed the children, bathed them and put them to bed; at William's request in the same bed. Usually one slept with him and the other child with her. After the children were asleep the quarrel started again and Sarah eventually felt so concerned for her own safety that she told Ingham that she was leaving and going to Liverpool. His reply was, "Very well, clear out!" As Sarah Rickard left the bungalow she noted that the children were still asleep; were they safe with William in that foul mood she wondered? He had always been a good father and he worshipped the little ones. Yes, she was sure that he would not harm them. She was frightened for herself but not for the children as she climbed aboard the bus taking her to Woodside

Some other 'bungalows' in the Fellowship Fields, Moreton

Ferry. In any case, Ingham knew where she was staying in Liverpool if he needed anything.

The next day nothing was seen of William Ingham and this odd circumstance led the owner of the land, Charles Burden, to force open the door late that afternoon. There was a strong smell of gas. Stretched out half-on the bed, partially covered by a blanket, were the bodies of Ingham and the two children. Post-mortem examination indicated that they had died late the night before.

The bungalow consisted of only two rooms; a bedroom and a kitchen cum living room. A bolt had been removed from the flimsy partition dividing the rooms and a gas tube had been attached to a gas ring in the kitchen and passed through the hole left by the detached bolt. All the apertures in the room had been securely sealed with pieces of cloth. Everything in the room was tidily arranged and several notes were discovered concerning debts to local tradesmen including a note to inform a dairyman, Mr Buchanan, that an account for £2.1/4d (£2.08) would be forwarded at an early date, and a half-crown coin (12.5p) was left on the table to pay Mr Bridge, the coalman. There was no doubt that William Ingham had been in full possession of his faculties as he planned his and his children's demise.

The West Cheshire Coroner, Mr JC Bate, held an enquiry in the Fellowship Hall into the tragic circumstances; returning a verdict of wilful murder against Ingham in respect of the two children and an inevitable verdict of suicide against Ingham himself.

Mrs Sarah Ingham was brought from Beeston to identify the body of her husband. Sarah Rickard, dressed in a dark blue coat and a black hat, testified that she had identified the bodies of her two young children. She was visibly upset and broke down several times during the enquiry. When questioned about their marital difficulties she admitted that Ingham had on several occasions before threatened to commit suicide. On the evening that she left the bungalow the children had been fast asleep. "I was not worried - I had left them with him before," she said. Questioned about the argument that night she stated that Ingham had asked her if she would change her ways but she had not known what he meant. "If we are to be happy, it's you who will have to change your ways," she had told him.

"How was the house kept - where did the money come from?" inquired the Coroner. "William sold and pawned things and he told me that he sometimes got money from his wife." "Why did you leave him that night?" "I was afraid of what he might do to me but I was not afraid for the children; he would not touch the children - he loved them."

Nevertheless, in desperation at his plight, William Ingham deliberately asphyxiated himself and his beloved children. Was it just lack of money that prompted this dreadful act or was there also an element of love, a desire to protect his children from any further distress. What went through his mind in the dark hours after Sarah left him we shall never know.

Chapter eight

MOTHER REDCAP'S

All ye that are weary come in and take rest,
Our eggs and our ham they are of the best,
Our ale and our porter are likewise the same,
Step in if you please and give 'em a name.

Mother Redcap

The original *Mother Redcap's Inn* stood on the Egremont Promenade between Caithness Drive and Lincoln Drive. It had also been known over the years as: *Red House, The Halfway House, The White House and Seabank Nook.* The building was burnt down in 1888 and replaced with its more modern Victorian structure. This in turn was demolished in 1974 and the replacement is known as *Mother Redcap's Nursing Home.* The only remains of the original *Mother Redcap's* are part of the wall fronting the Esplanade.

The house was erected in about 1595 on a piece of the moor just above high-water mark and at the time it was built it was said to be the only building on the river front between the old Seacombe Ferry boat house and New Brighton. The first owners were the Mainwaring family, later passing ownership to their relatives, the Davis family. The house became a tavern in the 1770s and was much frequented by the privateers, one of which was the 16 gun *Redcap.* In 1862 it was purchased by a Mrs Maddock and the licence was cancelled with the public house that had existed for all those years becoming a private residence.

It was built of red free stone with walls nearly three feet thick and had two mullioned lower front windows. The outside was at one time covered with thick planks from wrecked ships but eventually these rotted and fell off leaving the bare stone walls. But the most significant thing about the building was the front door and what was immediately behind it. The original door was of five inch thick solid oak with studding of square headed nails and there were iron slots to allow those inside to slide heavy wooden bars across the door. Just behind the front door on the inside was a trapdoor into the cellar with a rough wooden lid hinged in such a way that the forcing of the front door would withdraw the bolt of the trapdoor allowing any intruder to fall eight or nine feet into the cellar below. The cellar was also used for storage and at the back of the cellar were some stone steps rising to a passage leading to the back of the house on the south side - a useful and well thought out escape route. The old kitchen of the house led directly into the open backyard where there was a dry well about twelve feet deep. In the west wall of the well was a hole leading into a passage which probably joined another tunnel from the south side of the house where there was a large cave. The entrance to this cave was made to look like the steps down a well but much of the area of the yard was in fact a large underground cavity covered in flagstones supported by wooden beams. These flagstones were then covered with coal which was retailed from the premises, a few barrels of the strong, home-brewed ale for which the establishment was famous and, to complete the camouflage,

Mother Redcap's painted in 1857

a large heap of horse manure. From one end of the cave a tunnel ran to a concealed opening in a ditch about halfway up what is now Lincoln Drive. At the opening was a large willow tree which not only disguised the entrance but afforded a remarkably good view of the river entrance from its higher branches.

Inside the house the beams on either side of the fireplace were of old oak and the chimney breasts were enormous in size; the two ground floor rooms possessed chimney cavities with removable entrances from the top of the breasts inside the flues. The windows mentioned earlier had slots on either side so that strong shutters could be fitted. In the south room one wall had a cavity just large enough to conceal a small man and there were other covered spaces around the house where it was said that prize-money and some of the proceeds of 'wrecking' were hidden. Mother Redcap's was a veritable fortress.

In front of the house was a coarse pebble strand and two side stone walls ran from the north and south ends of the house down to the river. The north wall formed a good shelter for boats stored on its south side and this wall could be raised in height by the addition of sliding boards between thick posts. On the strand was a wooden flagstaff topped by a plain wooden vane; the vane itself was fixed and did not rotate with the wind but was turned from the base. This was used by the smugglers for signalling. If the vane pointed towards the house it meant 'Come on', and if pointed away it meant 'Keep off'.

In a book describing the activities of the Pressgang about 1797 written by Stonehouse in 1863 the following extract reveals more of the activities at Mother Redcap's:

"The men used to get across the water to Cheshire to hide until their ships were ready to sail. Near Egremont, on the shore, there used to be a little, low public house known as Mother Redcap's, from the fact of the owner always wearing a red hood or cap.

At the time there were no inner walls to divide the room on the upper floor, but only a few screens put up of about seven or eight feet in height

Mother Redcap's

to form compartments. The roof was not lathed or plastered and the joists and timbers were all open to view. Mother Redcap was a great favourite with the sailor men, and had their entire confidence. She had hiding places for any number. There is a tradition that the caves at the Red Noses communicated with Mother Redcap's. The men used, on returning from their voyages, to deposit with her their pay and prize-money until they wanted it. It was commonly believed that Mother Redcap had in her possession enormous sums of money hidden or put away somewhere, but where that somewhere was, it was never known, for at her death very little property was found in her possession although only a few days before she died a rich prize was brought into Liverpool which yielded every sailor on board at least £1000. Mother Redcap's was swarming with sailors belonging to the privateer directly after the vessel had come into port, and it was known that the lady had received a good deal of prize-money on their account, yet none of it was ever discovered."

In about 1850 a quantity of spade ace guineas was found in a cavity at Seacombe (Guinea Gap was named after this haul); perhaps this was part of a smuggler's hoard and could there still be a treasure trove to be found around those parts?

Mother Redcap was described as a comely, fresh-faced, Cheshire-spoken woman and at one time had a niece to help her. Curiously, considering all the attempts Mother Redcap had made to avoid the attentions of the authorities, the niece eventually married a customs officer!

Mother Redcap's painted in 1888

Chapter nine

FREDERICK KRUEGER -
THE WALLASEY HERMIT

Gotthold Johann Friedrick Krueger, who had been known locally as Frederick Krueger, the Wallasey Hermit, was found dead in his hut in a field adjoining Green Lane, Wallasey on 8 March 1909 by a labourer, Charles Webster of 2 Russell Road. He had lived in the area for up to 30 years and although everyone knew who he was, few knew much about him.

At the inquest some of his past was revealed. He was born in Mecklenburg about 1848 and his family was said to have been on the personal staff of the King of Prussia. He had graduated at Rostock, Munich and Leipzig Universities; was a Greek and Latin scholar as well as being fluent in English, French and Italian; not only a brilliant musician - a concert pianist of some note - but also a composer of some repute; had practised law in Germany; and had been a member of the German Diplomatic Corps where he was supposed to have gone to Peking to represent his country but came to England instead.

It was thought that he had lived in the Wallasey Village area for about 30 years, spending the last 20 years as a recluse living in a corrugated-iron hut on the Wallasey Golf Club links, off Green Lane. He apparently had no relatives in England and his main source of income was a small allowance from Germany. This was barely enough to maintain him but some locals, feeling an affection for him, gave him money out of charity. Probably the only person he was in direct contact with was Samuel Howard, market gardener of Green Lane, Wallasey, at whose address Krueger used to receive any mail. He was also in the habit of calling on the market gardener two or three times a week for fresh water.

When Wallasey Golf Club was founded and laid out in 1891, Krueger was already living on the site of the new course and his garden became an out of bounds for the 8th hole. This lasted until 1953 when the rule was abandoned.

On Monday 8 March at 8am, Charles Webster, who was working in a field near Krueger's hut and hadn't seen the hermit for some time, knocked

Frederick Krueger - the Wallasey Hermit

at his door. Receiving no answer but seeing what he thought was a body lying on the floor, he called at the police station. PC Robert Gilpin, stationed at Wallasey, went with Webster and breaking down the door found the hermit in a kneeling position, dead. Very few people had seen inside the hut which was 15ft long, 6ft wide, 12 ft high and partitioned into three. There was an extensive library including classical subjects in Latin and Greek, and also music by Wagner, Mozart and Krueger himself. However, it was a total clutter.

Removing the body to the Poulton Reading Room in Limekiln Lane was a problem as they had to keep Krueger's five retriever dogs at bay. The corpse was in a very dirty condition and although there were no marks of violence, the Coroner stated that the skin on the left cheek and by the bridge of the nose had been gnawed by rats and that the deceased had suffered from a strangulated hernia and peritonitis, which was the cause of death. The deceased had been dead for three to four days.

Everyone talked about the hermit of Wallasey, who was described as being very hunched, a Bohemian type with a drooping moustache, but very few knew him. He was heard to say that he had no friends and wished to exist alone and all he desired was the right to pass his days in study and contemplation. Why did this highly educated and talented man abandon his cultured world for a country where he had no connections and live the life of a recluse? The Wallasey Villagers clubbed together to pay for a proper funeral, so that he would not have to be buried in a pauper's grave. Frederick Krueger's secret died with him in a small ramshackle hut in Wallasey.

The funeral procession of the 'Hermit of Wallasey' 13 March 1909

Chapter ten

Dr CRIPPEN
The Story of the Mild Murderer
and
THE MERSEYSIDE CONNECTIONS

Who would have guessed that the dapper little man with a drooping moustache and gold-rimmed spectacles giving a medical lecture at New Brighton in 1907 would become one of the most notorious men of this century?

Dr Hawley Harvey Crippen's lecture on 'Electrical Massage for Rheumatism' at the Assembly Rooms in Albion Street, New Brighton was reported as being well received. The Assembly Rooms were a popular venue for socials and meetings. It was here that Mrs Pankhurst addressed an audience on the suffragette movement in October 1910 - the same month that Dr Crippen stood trial for the murder of his wife.

Hawley Harvey Crippen, an American homoeopathic doctor married Cora Turner (real name Kunigunde Mackamotzki), an attractive Polish-German girl, in Jersey City in 1892. His wife was to recognise that there was no money to be made as a doctor of homoeopathic medicine, so persuaded him to become a 'quack' doctor. In 1894 he joined Munyon's Remedies, a patent medicine company (its main claim to fame was a cure for piles). In 1897 the company sent him to open an office in London on a salary of $10,000.

Cora had ambitions to take the London stage by storm and took on the stage name of Belle Elmore. Crippen acted as her manager but due to her limited talent, she received few music hall or smoking concert engagements. However, following the publicity for one of her performances, Munyon

Dr Crippen and the Merseyside Connections

found out that Crippen was the manager of a music hall singer, so fired him although a few years later he acted as an agent for Munyons.

Off stage Cora was better received by the theatrical fraternity and attained the position of treasurer to the Music Hall Ladies' Guild. Having once been a mistress to a wealthy businessman in America, her taste for expensive clothes and jewellery meant that her husband had to find ways of funding her demands.

Crippen took on other employment involving medically orientated ventures including being a 'consultant physician' for Drouets Institute for the Deaf, a dubious mail-order company he joined in 1901 (see advertisement on next page), which eventually went bankrupt. This was a confidence trick from France with the company's expensive London offices being located in Regents Park Road from where they targeted the less well off who were more gullible. Patches were stuck onto the skin behind the ear and were claimed to cure most hearing problems by their penetrating powers - these claims of course was not true.

It was here that he met Ethel Le Neve, a 17 year old typist. She was a hypochondriac who was probably unable to gain the attentions of someone of her own age as she had a deformed foot and so she turned to the much older man. It was, perhaps, the dominating characters of both Cora and Ethel that attracted Crippen as he was a masochist when it came to his relationships with women. Is this why he put up with Cora sleeping with some of the lodgers they took in, in order to make ends meet?

With the bankrupt stock purchased from Drouets, Crippen and Le Neve, started the Aural Remedies Company, relabelling some of Drouet's (doubtful) remedies. This brought them into contact with an unsavoury character, Eddie Marr, but Ethel influenced Crippen away from patent medicines into dentistry with her as his assistant. They set up as "The Yale Tooth Specialists - American Dentists", in partnership with a young American, Dr Gilbert Rylance, who had gained a dentistry degree in New Zealand. Despite having no dentistry qualifications, Crippen carried out

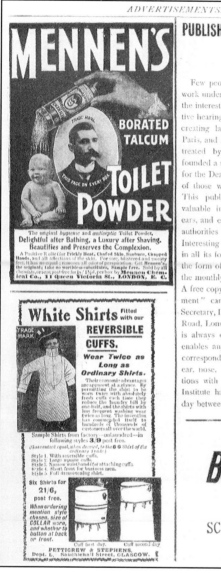

This page of advertisements, which is taken from a 1902 Pearsons *magazine, includes one for Druets Institute [for the Deaf], the company Crippen worked for at that time. This advertisement, which was made to look like a feature and not an advertisement, was probably the work of Crippen who had gained experience of the mail order 'quack' cures from working with Munyon's. Ironically, one of the main features in this publication was Marconi's new wireless system - which was to prove the invention which led to Crippen's capture and subsequent conviction!*

the extractions! It was at this stage that Ethel became pregnant. She was determined to have the baby and force Crippen to split with his wife.

Cora led a double life - on the one hand as the charming Belle Elmore (her stage name) beloved by her many theatrical friends, including the famous Marie Lloyd, and on the other hand ruling her husband with a rod of iron, treating him with contempt, bullying and tormenting him. Her friends did not like her husband as they thought he was a weak character and a sponger. When she found out that he was having an affair with a much younger woman she mocked and teased him. This affair between Crippen, aged 48, and Ethel Le Neve, who was half his age, was the only happiness in his life. When Cora, who was unable to have children due to an ovariectomy some years previously found out that Ethel was pregnant, she threatened to take all their money and leave Crippen penniless. However, Ethel suffered a miscarriage and Cora never carried out her threat. This would have been an ideal time for Crippen to leave Cora for Ethel, the woman he loved, but he did not and carried on seeing Ethel by day and sleeping at night under the same roof, albeit in separate bedrooms, with Cora.

Crippen was able to take all the torment and abuse from his wife aimed at him personally, but it was when she started making comments about Ethel that he probably decided to take steps to get rid of her. On 17 January 1910 he purchased five grains of an obscure poison, hyoscine hydrobromide, from the chemist in New Oxford Street in London whom he bought his medicines from in connection with his homoeopathetic preparations. Some say that it was possible that Ethel either knew of her lover's intent to kill his wife or even helped to plan it, but this is only speculation.

The Crippens invited some of Cora's music-hall friends, Mr & Mrs Martinetti, for dinner on 31 January 1910, but although Mr Martinetti was not well, Crippen insisted they came - would his plans have been spoilt if they had not come? When leaving at about 1.30am Cora waved goodbye to them. They were the last people, other than her husband, to see her alive. Had Crippen already poisoned his wife when the Martinetti's were there? If not, then he must have administered it in the early hours of that day and buried her mutilated body under the cellar floor of their house at 39 Hilldrop Crescent, Holloway and disposed of the rest. Later in the day he pawned some of Cora's jewellery and Ethel stayed at Hilldrop Crescent for the first time the following night, moving in permanently some six weeks later.

Crippen forged a letter from his wife to the guild resigning her membership stating that she had to go to America due to a family illness. After this, Belle's theatrical friends became suspicious, initially because she had left in such haste without telling any of them and then even more so when Crippen attended the Variety Artist's Charity Ball on 20 February, three weeks later, escorted by Ethel Le Neve. She was wearing one of Belle's favourite pieces of jewellery, a 'rising sun' diamond brooch. This caused Belle's friends to become even more curious about her sudden disappearance as they were sure that she would not have approved of Ethel wearing her brooch.

Following a rumour he spread that Cora was dangerously ill in America with pneumonia, Crippen, on his way to Dieppe with Ethel for their 'honeymoon', sent a cable to the Martinettis from Victoria Station on 24 March stating, 'Belle died yesterday at six o'clock'. He later dealt successfully with the questions from Cora's inquisitive friends about the details of her death and funeral arrangements.

The couple continued to live at Hilldrop Crescent with Ethel wearing Cora's expensive jewellery and furs. Friends of Cora's went to Scotland Yard with their suspicions, following her mysterious disappearance, but the police did not have enough evidence to make an arrest. Determined to get to the bottom of the mystery, some other friends when visiting Los Angeles on a business trip in May made enquiries to the authorities who could find no death records for either Cora Crippen or Belle Elmore. So upon returning home they took their further evidence to Scotland Yard.

This started a police enquiry into Cora's disappearance led by Chief

Dr Crippen and the Merseyside Connections

Inspector Walter Dew who visited Crippen at work on 8 July. Crippen admitted that he had lied and made up a convincing story about Cora still being alive, running away to join her American lover, and agreed to a search of 39 Hilldrop Crescent by Inspector Dew. Finding nothing suspicious, the inspector felt sorry for the pathetic man and promised to circulate Cora's description to the American Press. This he did.

At this point Crippen made his worst error of judgement. Wrongly thinking that the police were on to him, he panicked and decided to flee the country with Ethel. For when the inspector returned the next day over some minor detail and found both the office and house empty, with signs of a hurried departure, he decided to circulate the couple's pictures and descriptions.

Inspector Dew aided by Detective Sergeant Mitchell started to search the house and dig up the garden and on the third day, the 13 July, their suspicions were confirmed when the Inspector discovered part of a body buried in a shallow grave under the coal cellar floor. Crippen had made further errors. He had filleted the body and disposed of the skull, limbs and bones possibly by burning them on a fire. Then he treated the fleshy remains of the body with slaked lime, which preserves human flesh, instead of quicklime which would have destroyed any evidence. The torso was then buried but because the body had not decomposed the police were able to confirm that the scar on the abdomen was similar to one on Cora Crippen. Police also found traces of hyoscine in the organs. Another mistake, as he later learned, was that it was wrapped in a pyjama jacket labelled 'Shirtmakers, Jones Brothers, Holloway'. On the 16 July warrants were issued for the arrest of Crippen and Le Neve for murder and mutilation with the story hitting the headlines in this country and on the continent.

The couple had in fact fled to Rotterdam and then on to Antwerp where they booked a passage to Canada. They boarded the *SS Montrose* bound for Canada on 20 July.

A young member of the staff of the Mission to Seamen in Antwerp at that time was Frank Davies, who was later to become the Vicar of St Paul's,

Dr Crippen and the Merseyside Connections

The MARCONI INTERNATIONAL MARINE COMMUNICATION COMPANY, Ltd

WATERGATE HOUSE, YORK BUILDINGS, ADELPHI, LONDON, WC..

Brookhaven 3.30pm

July 22nd

To: Piers Liverpool

3pm GMT Friday 130 miles West Lizard have strong suspicions that Crippen London Cellar Murderer and accomplice are amongst Saloon passengers moustache taken off growing beard accomplice dressed as boy voice manner and build undoubtedly a girl both travelling as Mr and Master Robinson

Kendall

This was the first message sent by wireless-telegraph to intercept a fugitive (see next page)

Seacombe 1926-1947 and then the Vicar of Frankby 1947-1960. Part of his duties was to visit the crews of ships docked in Antwerp. Members of the *Montrose* crew gave a concert in the Mission's Institute in Plein Van Schoonbech. The following day before the ship sailed for Canada, he visited the ship to wish the crew 'bon voyage' and then stood at the foot of the gangway watching the passengers boarding. Dr Crippen and Miss Le Neve must have passed within inches of him and he later said he might have been more sharp-eyed! However, this would not have been easy from pictures circularised in the press because Crippen's photograph was 20 years old. Also, he had removed his moustache, started to grow a beard, wore no spectacles and travelled as Mr John Philo Robinson with Le Neve disguised as his son, John.

A further mistake Crippen made was that on the morning that they fled he had sent his dental assistant out to buy some boy's clothes to fit Ethel. So the police already knew that Le Neve was probably disguised as a boy.

The observant commander, Captain Henry G Kendall from Harlech Road

Dr Crippen and the Merseyside Connections

in Blundellsands, Nr Liverpool, saw through the deception, mainly due to a chance sighting of 'father and son' holding hands. The captain was curious. In order to get a closer view of them, he invited the couple to dine with him and noted that the boy ate very delicately, spoke in a soft voice and had girlish mannerisms. Whereas Philo Robinson (Crippen had a cousin of that name) wore no glasses the observant captain noticed marks on the bridge of his nose caused by wearing them. His suspicions were further aroused when he thought that Crippen carried a revolver in his pocket. Having checked the photographs and description in the *Daily Mail*, which was offering a £100 reward for information leading to their arrest, and certain that they were the couple the police were looking for, he sent a radio-telegraph message to Scotland Yard via Liverpool - the first crime in which this new Marconi wireless system had been used to intercept a fugitive (*see previous page*).

Using this novel communication system, Captain Kendall was able to telegraph a daily report on Crippen and Le Neve's activities to the *Montreal Star* newspaper in Canada who in turn relayed the information back to England. The fleeing couple continued to enjoy the company of the captain oblivious to the fact that what they did or said would probably be read by a captive audience around the world the following morning!

Ironically Crippen heard the crackle of the wireless and according to Captain Kendall remarked; "What a marvelous invention it is! How priviledged we are to be alive in an age of such scientific miracles." He was later to learn the significance of Marconi's invention.

Inspector Dew followed the *SS Montrose* aboard the faster *SS Laurentic* which caught her up and the inspector boarded her on the morning of 31 July 1910 in the mouth of the St Lawrence River just 16 hours from Quebec. Crippen was surprised when Inspector Dew greeted him with: "Good morning Dr Crippen, I am Inspector Dew" Crippen replied : "Good morning Mr Dew." The inspector proceeded to their cabin to arrest Le Neve who then fainted. The Canadian police who accompanied the inspector arrested them and took them into custody awaiting extradition back to England. Journalists following the case waited alongside the *Montrose* in a pilot boat until the arrests were made were then allowed to board the ship and interview the unsuspecting passengers and crew.

After the two fugitives were arrested they were searched. Crippen was found to have two 'John Robinson' business cards in his pocket. The first read:

'I cannot stand the horror I go through every night any longer and as I see nothing ahead and money has come to an end, I have made up my mind to jump overboard tonight. I know I have spoiled your life but I'll hope some day you can learn to forgive me. Last words of love. Yours H'

The other card read:
'Shall we wait till tonight about 10 or 11? If not what time?.....

The first card was a suicide note to Ethel and the second fits into Crippen's story at the trial that he had bribed one of the crew to smuggle him ashore before the ship docked - was this note arranging the time Crippen was to leave the ship? - or were these messages meant to mislead the police?

The ship's surgeon was a Dr Spottiswoode who lived for many years in Seabank Road, Wallasey and afterwards he said that Crippen had had a bottle of poison in his possession on the ship. Whether or not he intended

SS Laurentic, *the ship that Inspector Dew used to catch the SS Montrose*

to administer it to himself it is not known - he did not have the opportunity to use it before he was taken into custody.

The extradition procedure from Canada took less than three weeks. Then the inspector and his two captives returned to Liverpool aboard the *SS Magantic*, sister ship to the *SS Laurentic* (both belonging to the White Star Line whose owner, J Bruce Ismay, lived at 'Dawpool', Thurstaston). Due to the publicity surrounding the arrests and in order to avoid the press and angry public who were waiting at Liverpool, docking at Birkenhead was considered, but this option was never followed.

The trial of Crippen began on 18 October and lasted five days with Crippen behaving with courteous dignity. His main hope of avoiding execution was to plead guilty due to mitigating circumstances but this would have required Ethel to be called as a witness - a situation he wanted to avoid, so he opted for a defence which would not involve the only love in his life. He was defended by Arthur Newton who was brilliant but unscrupulous. He was later to be sent to prison for forging Crippen's 'confessions' and selling them to a newspaper. Crippen refused to plead guilty and argued that the remains could have been buried in the cellar when he bought the house in 1905. However, an employee of the manufacturer of the pyjamas,

The SS Megantic, *the ship that brought Crippen and LeNeve back from Canada to Liverpool - seen here in the Mersey*

Dr Crippen and the Merseyside Connections

Jones Brothers, stated in court that the material the body was wrapped in had not been available before 1908 and that two pairs of this type had been delivered to Crippen in January 1909.

Forensic evidence played an important part in the conviction. Bernard Spilsbury (later Sir Bernard), who was to become the most famous pathologist of his day, made his first appearance in the witness-box at this trial. He proved the Crown's case that the scar on part of the torso corresponded with that of Cora's operation when one of her ovaries was removed. The defence pathologists originally contended that it was not a scar but a mark where the skin had folded. However, they eventually agreed that they were wrong. Later, in a letter to Ethel, Crippen wrote: 'Today at the appeal I realised more and more that the medical evidence for my defence was so mismanaged that it told against me rather than for me. . . .I am powerless now, and can do no more, but bow to the inevitable'.

It took the jury only 27 minutes to find Harvey Hawley Crippen guilty of wilful murder to which Crippen replied: "I still protest my innocence," and appealed against the conviction.

One of the mysteries of the case was why did Crippen kill his wife when he could have walked out of her life? Another puzzle was why did he dismember the body? Several theories of what happened after the Martinettis left 39 Dewdrop Crescent were put forward, one of the more likely was by Dr Ingleby Oddie, who worked with Richard Muir for the prosecution. His theory was that Crippen thought that if he poisoned his wife with hyoscine, it would appear that she had had a heart attack. But what he did not realise was that a large dose would not sedate her but make her hysterical. Witnesses stated that they heard screams and also a loud bang coming from the Crippen's house on the morning of the murder. In order to avoid being interrupted by neighbours Crippen had to silence his wife. It is known that he possessed a gun so he could have shot her through the head in her bedroom. Then he had to dispose of the body but Cora was a heavy woman and he was only slight. The solution was to move the corpse to the adjoining bathroom and dismember the body in the bath (Crippen admitted in court that he had attended a theoretical course of surgery). Getting rid of the body was then easier and the blood could be washed down the plug hole (the police found no trace of blood in the house). As this was not planned perhaps it became too much for him physically and not being able to get rid of all the body due to lack of time, he burned the head and limbs on a fire and buried the torso in a shallow grave in the coal cellar, covering it in slaked lime thinking it would decompose - but it did not.

Alternatively the Regent's Canal was only half a mile away or the reservoir was even nearer (Camelot House in Holloway now stands on the site of the reservoir) - and a few trips with weighted-down bags containing parts of her body could have been made to either place. However, this would have been far more risky than burning them and disposing of the remains in the dustbin, as he would have aroused suspicion if he had been seen or the police would probably have dredged the canal and reservoir. This is one part of the Crippen case that will always remain a mystery.

Crippen had always been anxious to clear Ethel's name and when her case came to court at the Old Bailey on 25 October she was charged as an accessory to murder after the fact. The trial only lasted one day and was dominated by a brilliant speech by her defence lawyer, FE Smith, old boy of Birkenhead School and later to become Lord Birkenhead. Called to the Bar in 1899 he was described as handsome, witty and flamboyant. He became the youngest King's Council in Britain, Lord Chancellor, Solicitor General, Attorney General, Secretary of State for India - all before he was 53. Le Neve had asked her solicitors to instruct F.E. (Smith) to defend her.

F.E. was so sure of a favourable outcome, that he called for no evidence on Ethel's behalf explaining to the jury that she had gone through enough and he would not put a young, inexperienced woman with poor health in the box (she was in fact 27 at the time!). Taking the jury through a scenario of Ethel being the innocent working girl he asked them if she would have worn the 'rising sun' brooch to the charity ball knowing that the owner

FE Smith, an old boy of Birkenhead School, successfully defended Ethel Le Neve (see previous page)

had been murdered. He went on to ask the jury if they could really believe that Crippen would take such care to hide all the traces of murder, then risk the 'aversion, revulsion and disgust' of a young nervous woman by telling her: "This is how I treated the woman who last shared my home, and I invite you to come and share it with me now."

It took the jury only 20 minutes to find her not guilty and she was discharged. F.E. was convinced of her innocence and later wrote of the case: 'Frail she was, and of submissive temperament, but not an accomplice in murder, or an ally in its concealment.' After the trial the Lord Chief Justice remarked to F.E. that he should have put Ethel in the box - F.E. replied: "No, I knew what she would say - you did not."

Crippen was pleased with the outcome of her case and remained hopeful of his appeal. This was evident from the letters he wrote from prison to Ethel between 28 October and 5 November when his unsuccessful appeal was heard. He continued writing the letters up to 22 November but despite 15,000 signatures for a reprieve, on 23 November 1910 he was hanged at Pentonville Prison and was buried in an unmarked grave in the prison yard. His last request, that Ethel's letters and photograph be buried with him, was carried out.

Ethel escaped further publicity by emigrating aboard the *Majestic* via New York to Toronto, Canada. She returned to her native England in 1916 to nurse her dying sister Nina. She met her husband-to-be, Stanley Smith, who was said to resemble Crippen, at her place of work where she was a typist. In 1954 her real identity was discovered by novelist, Ursula Bloom who wrote a fictional novel based on Ethel Le Neve called *The Girl Who Loved Crippen*. Through this publication she was to meet Ethel's brother and via him Ethel, who by this time had been widowed. Miss Bloom and Ethel became good friends over the years but none of the secrets of Hilldrop Crescent were ever disclosed - only that nobody, outside her blood relatives, knew her real identity, not even her husband or two children. Ethel Le Neve died in obscurity in 1967 aged 84.

Number 39 Hilldrop Crescent was war-damaged and, along with its neighbours, was demolished and Margaret Bonfield House, a block of flats, was built on the site. It is said that on the 31 January the ghost of Dr Crippen still walks in the shadows of Hilldrop Crescent.

A strange event occurred aboard the *SS Megantic* when a local steward fell asleep on one of the bunks in the second-class cabins. He awoke screaming and in a cold sweat. A colleague rushed in, asked what all the noise was about and upon hearing about the nightmare said: "This is the bunk that Dr Crippen slept in when he was brought home to stand trial last year."

Cora Crippen's jewellery was sold at auction in London in 1911. Mr Charles Fry, a well known local jeweller, pawnbroker and house furnisher who had branches in Egremont, Liscard and New Brighton, purchased the 'rising sun', probably the most famous of Cora's pieces. Large numbers of people were attracted to view the item which he displayed in the window of his Liscard Road branch, advertising the fact that this was one of the jewels that Ethel Le Neve had worn.

Many of those who attended the lecture at New Brighton in 1907, given by the mild, pleasant and courteous Dr Crippen, would have followed the case avidly, as did most of the world, and might have been forgiven for thinking that it was Cora Crippen who was the villain of the piece - driving her husband beyond the bounds of human dignity - into the crime for which they both paid with their lives.

Chapter eleven

SKELETON IN SEACOMBE

On a miserable Thursday morning in November 1907 a gruesome discovery was made in a pit in a field immediately opposite the old Police Station in Liscard Road, Seacombe which was situated beween Clarendon Road and Falkland Road. The land was being laid out for building purposes and the builder, Mr C Warren of Seacombe, instructed his men to drain the water from the pit preparatory to its being filled up. When the water had been run off the workers were horrified to find a quantity of human bones at the bottom of the pit. They were sure that they were the skeleton of a man. The bones had the appearance of having been in the water for some years and there was no sign of flesh or clothing. The police were informed and the bones removed to Seacombe Ferry Mortuary for examination. An inquest was to be held some days later by the West Cheshire Coroner but the day before the inquest the police had the answer to the mystery.

Some ten years before a Dr Murray Laffan had resided at No 1 Clarendon Road on the corner of Liscard Road. When he moved from the house he left behind in a cupboard a man's skeleton which he had used for anatomical reference. Later the house was occupied by the Vicar of Egremont, the Rev OTL Crossley, and his house-keeper, in preparing the house for his residence, came across the bones in the cupboard. Not knowing what to do with the bones she had put them in a sack and hurled the sack into the pit where they were to be found years later.

Chapter twelve

THE LUSITANIA RIOTS IN BIRKENHEAD

The *Lusitania* was built by John Brown of Clydebank and launched in 1907 at a cost of £1.3m, she weighed 32,500 tons and was 706ft long. The Cunard ship was sunk off Ireland on Friday 7 May 1915 by a torpedo from a German submarine and because there were many Merseysiders among the 1,198 who lost their lives, anti-German riots broke out in Liverpool, Bootle, Wallasey and Birkenhead. The rioting began in Liverpool on Saturday evening 8 May as the result, not only of the general feeling of hatred against the Germans, but in certain areas due to the many local crew members who had perished with the ship. German or Austrian named businesses were targeted by the angry crowds with the contents of many of them thrown onto the street and set on fire.

Following the rioting in Liverpool on Saturday and Sunday against the

The Lusitania at the Liverpool Landing Stage c1911

German and Austrian businesses for fear that it would spread across the Mersey, public houses in Birkenhead were closed at 6pm on Monday evening following the advice of its Chief Constable, Edward Parker. Also the most vulnerable people in Birkenhead were warned by the police of the impending danger and had left the area. This was sound advice for, as predicted, the trouble started on Monday evening 10 May.

The first attack in Birkenhead was on a pork butcher's shop belonging to John Swarb at 49 Watson Street. The crowd began to stone the windows at which time the police tried to intervene, with Superintendent Jones and Inspectors Bebbington and Howard in attendance, but due to the increasing numbers they were powerless and soon all the shop windows and those above were broken. Every effort was made by the police to restrain the crowd, with some of them being hit by stones aimed at the windows, but the mob was bent on destruction and soon the police were overpowered and the contents of the shop were thrown into the roadway amid much cheering.

Before the wrecking in Watson Street was over a large body of the crowd made off to 135 Price Street, the pork butcher's shop of Charles Dashley,

Charles Dashley's shop in Oxton Road, boarded up after the attack on Monday (see this page)

who also had a shop Oxton Road. The Price Street shop came under the same sort of attack as at John Swarb's and soon every pane of glass was broken, the contents of the shop were ransacked and pitched out onto the street. The spirit of the riot quickly spread and the next target was Charles Dashley's other shop in Oxton road (*see previous page*). This according to the police was the worst attack, mainly due to the rioters from Price Street and Watson Street being joined by others also bent on destruction. About 20 policemen, including Inspector Bebbington, positioned themselves in strategic places to hold back the mob which after an hour was estimated in thousands and angry shouts against the Germans were heard everywhere. Although the police were helped by a number of soldiers, eventually they were overwhelmed by a growing crowd. As before, all the shop windows and those above were broken and the wrecking of the shop began. The contents of the shop were pitched into the street including hams, pieces of pork, sausages, pickles, shopfittings, cash books and anything else which came to hand. The rioters then threw out the contents of the upstairs rooms and the shop shutters were thrown onto the pile in the road which was then set alight. One policeman had to be taken to hospital with a bad cut; then the fire brigade arrived and proceeded to extinguish the fire. By this time the crowd seemed satisfied and there being no bad feelings towards the police or fire brigade, the crowd dispersed without any arrests. If they had detained any of the rioters then this would undoubtedly have led to more serious disorder and led to adjoining properties being attacked.

Quite early in the rioting another pork butcher's shop, this one in the name of Otto Krook, was attacked on the corner of Dacre Street and Camden Street. The police had no warning about this attack, especially as it was known that the owners had a son serving in the British Army. The crowd broke every pane of glass and then set about the inside of the premises where they found a picture of King George and Queen Mary downstairs but in an upstairs room they thought they had found a picture of the Kaiser which was held out of a bedroom window (*see page 86*). Immediately the wrecking became more furious culminating in a valuable piano being thrown out of the upstairs window and smashing into pieces in the roadway below. This was burned in the street, together with other items from the premises,

The Lusitania Riots in Birkenhead

The crowd viewing the damage done to the private residence of August Hessler on the corner of Church Street and Pilgrim Street (see next page)

with the fire brigade and police arriving and doing their best to quell the fire and the disorder continuing.

The trouble in Oxton Road finished about 9.30pm but directly afterwards there were further outbreaks in the quiet neighbourhood of Woodchurch Road where two shops were attacked. Frederick Miller's boot repair shop at No 5 and Miss Bendix's milliner and draper shop at No 41, on the corner of Glover Street. The police arrived but were unable to stop the windows of both premises being broken. There was much sympathy, particularly with the Bendix family who were regarded locally as quiet, respectable people and although their father was of German origin he had lived in this country for a long time. Looting went on at both shops and the next day some customers of Frederick Miller found that their boots left for repair had disappeared!

A section of the crowd in Oxton Road was stirred by a cry of "Pilgrim Street" and were joined on the way there by others. Their target was a

The Lusitania Riots in Birkenhead

The police were unable to control the large crowds outside Henry Young's sweet shop in Bedford Road (see this page)

large private house owned by August Hessler at No 2, on the corner of Church Street. He was the owner of Hessler & Son, fruiterers and potato merchants. The majority of windows, except for some on the third floor, were broken. Their neighbours at 77 Church Street displayed national flags (*see picture on previous page*) to show their allegance to their country and to ensure that their house did not get attacked by mistake.

Large crowds gathered outside the sweet shop belonging to Henry Young at 406 New Chester Road and threw missiles against the plate-glass windows, which clattered down with a crash. The occupants had been pre-warned of the trouble and had put the stock beyond the reach of the mob which consisted of many women and children. However, all the fittings were destroyed. A number of constables had been drafted in to control the crowds but were powerless. Another shop owned by Henry Young at 23 Bedford Road, Rock Ferry was given similar treatment but the stock had not been removed from the shop. Sweets were showered from the shop after the windows had been broken and again the police were unable to control the large crowd, (*see picture on this page which gives an indication of the problems that the police encountered*).

The Lusitania Riots in Birkenhead

Following the grave disturbances in Birkenhead on Monday evening and rumours that further attacks were to take place on Tuesday, action was taken by the police. A large number of the Birkenhead special constables were called up for duty (during the riots 436 special constables were enrolled) and public houses were closed at 2pm on Tuesday. The rioting on Tuesday, although destructive, was not as serious as on Monday because all of the obvious targets had been severely dealt with by then and the fact it rained heavily at about 8.30pm dampened the spirits of the rioters. Those looking for trouble were relying on the flimsiest of hearsay evidence and in some cases there was no evidence at all - but a good excuse for looting.

Problems started at lunchtime when stones were thrown at a hairdresser's shop in Oxton named Strauss. Emile Strauss was a German and had been interned but his wife, who was looking after the business at 12 Oxton Road, was born and bred in Yorkshire. She had been advised to leave which luckily she did for all the shop windows were broken as were the fittings and the place was left a total wreck. Another hairdresser's establishment in Balls Road was attacked and again all the windows were smashed.

It was rumoured that a family living in Price Street, with an English name, had German connections and that the wife had been overheard to say something pro German the previous evening. Based on this hearsay a mob gathered outside their house at 7pm and burst open the front door. In a very short space of time the house was ransacked with a piano and other furniture thrown into the street. An attempt to set fire to the premises was partially successful but the fire had been put out by the time the fire brigade arrived. Prior to this trouble, boys had hurled stones through a chip shop window in Price Street said to have been run by a German.

The police held back the crowd outside Woodson's grocery shop in Conway Street for some time but they were determined to wreck the store, even though there were no German connections and a Union Jack was displayed at their Grange Road branch (*see pages 86/87*). Shortly after 8.30pm a rush was made for the shop and the police were overcome. The windows were smashed in and within a few minutes looting began on a large scale.

The Lusitania Riots in Birkenhead

Men and women were rushing out of the shop with biscuit tins, ornaments and provisions of every kind. The police were very tactful and later got the crowd under control and successfully closed the shop.

Even private residences were at risk. One such was that of Mr Charles Gostenhoffer of 6 Wexford Road. A large crowd, estimated to be in excess of 1,000, gathered outside or near to his home but the police were present in force. Mr Cecil Holden did good service by appealing to the crowd to be sensible and go away. A few stones were thrown, one hitting a policeman, but the crowd dispersed.

There were some disgraceful scenes at the south end of the town where a large crowd assembled in New Chester Road, opposite the premises of Mr R Cundall, pork butcher, who was said to be a British citizen. He had received a warning from the police that there might be trouble so he had removed his stock from the premises and had left with his family. His assistant tried to keep the crowd back and when the window was broken and the police moved in, he calmly removed what was left from the shop which could have been looted. Further down New Chester Road, another crowd, mainly of boys, stoned a boot-repairer's establishment. However, not much damage was done and as it started to rain heavily the crowd broke up.

Further damage was done to property owned by seemingly innocent people including an attack by a crowd of mainly women and young boys on the fried fish dealer's shop of Mr Thomas Lincoln at 220 Price Street. Mr & Mrs Lincoln abandoned the premises to them and very soon it was wrecked. The furniture was turfed into the road and tablecloths were used to carry away stolen clocks and other items. A fire was lit with newspapers and would have taken hold if two naval officers and a policeman had not arrived at that moment. A neighbour said that neither of the Lincolns was German but their only offence was that they were alleged to have traded with Germans. The crowd having achieved their objective here moved on, singing, cheering and jeering, to 14 Massey Street, the home of Mr & Mrs George Murray. He was a fireman and English but she was said to be a German. Here again all the windows were smashed, the contents thrown into the

The Lusitania Riots in Birkenhead

street and set alight. A policeman who lived next door was able to extinguish the fire and drive away the marauders who moved on to 151 Livingstone Street, the home of John Swarb whose shop was attacked on Monday (*see page 79*). The police were able to keep them at bay and only a few windows were broken from long range. The next attack was at the home of Miss Mary Fuchs, 57 Bidston Avenue and again the crowd had to be content with some broken windows. Miss Fuchs apparently fainted and some said she was dying. This clearly upset the crowd which was then reported to have dispersed.

On the Tuesday, one of the first cases arising out of the riots from the previous day was heard by Mr TL Dodds (presiding) and Mr LC Elmslie. It involved Patrick Morris of 37 Russell Street who was charged with doing wilful damage to a plate-glass window worth £8, the property of John Swarb of 49 Watson Street *(see page 79)*. Following evidence from witnesses it was established that Morris had thrown the stone that had broken the window. A remand for a week was ordered with bail being allowed.

The Chairman in conclusion said :

"We have to say to you and to others that after making every allowance for the national indignation, at one of the most awful crimes, we cannot allow you to take the law into your own hands. It is foolish (to say nothing about the criminality of the case) because by this rowdyism you are simply inviting retaliation on English people in Germany. If when the end comes and Germany will be called upon to account for the awful crime of sinking the Lusitania and the loss of nearly 1,100 innocent lives with the ship, then the rowdyism in Birkenhead and other cities will be pleaded in mitigation of judgement. Also, presumably the damage inflicted will have to be made good by the ratepayers. The proper thing to do is to restrain your indignation and wait. We hope that there will be no repetition of these regrettable scenes."

There was no renewal of the anti-German street riots on Wednesday or the following days. The damage caused by the riots was cleared up from the streets and the wrecked properties were boarded up with at least one policeman being stationed outside each of these premises. The public houses remained closed until Saturday. Damage done in the riots was to be paid out of public rates - this was provided for by the Riots (Damage) Act of 1886. The ratepayers were not liable in the case of proved German citizens - in those cases the state was liable.

The aftermath of the riots produced much evidence that many of the properties attacked had no connection with Germany or Austria. Otto Krook Jnr. sent a letter to a local newspaper on 19 May stating that his father had lived in Camden Street for 18 years and his mother had lived in England since she was a young girl. He (their son) was born in England and was currently serving in the British army. The picture of the Kaiser which was found on their property was in fact a picture of his grand father, a Russian-Finn (*see page 80*).

Another letter was sent by Wilhelmine Bendix following the damage done to her shop (*see page 81*) which denied rumours being circulated that she had five brothers and three brothers-in-law all serving in the German army and that one brother was a German spy. She did in fact have only one brother who had been born in Liverpool and had no connections with Germany, three of her sisters were all married to British citizens and the other three sisters helped her in the shop.

During the riots some shopkeepers placed notices outside their shops denying any connection with Germany. One was Mr A Appleton, pawnbroker of 263 Old Chester Road, whose notice read: 'It is rumoured that I am a German. I am not'. He then proceeded to give a detailed account of his pedigree and ended the notice by saying: '£25 reward if proved false'. Another innocent victim was Mr E Wood of Woodson's stores. His Conway Street branch had been wrecked and looted (*see page 83*) and his Grange Road and Rock Ferry shops suffered slight damage so he took an advertisement in a local paper for several weeks after the rioting. It offered £1,000 reward to anyone proving that any of his family were German (*see opposite*).

The Lusitania Riots in Birkenhead

By the end of the week a large number of people had charges of looting and rioting brought against them. Fines of 20 shillings (one pound) or 11 days imprisonment were imposed on many of them. Although the damage caused by the rioters in Birkenhead was both destructive and widespread, it was much greater in Liverpool where over 200 shops and houses were wrecked or damaged by the 'Lusitania Riots' at an estimated value of £40,000 - £50,000, whereas in Birkenhead only 24 shops or houses were attacked.

WOODSON'S HARD LINES
£1,000 REWARD

The above amount will be paid to any person who can prove that the statements being circulated that Mr Wood or any of his family are German

---

Miss Wood is at present a nurse in a Red Cross hospital in France and has been since the commencement of war in August

---

Mr E Wood Junior late of 146 Grange Road branch shop is in training with the Liverpool 1st 'Pals' Battalion
NONE OF OUR EMPLOYEES ARE GERMAN

We thank all our good friends for the kind sympathy extended to us, also for the patronage for the past 12 years in the district, and hope the same will be extended to us in the future

---

WOODSONS STORES
E WOOD & SONS,
SOLE PROPRIETORS

BIBLIOGRAPHY

Boumphrey, Ian & Marilyn, *Yesterday's Wirral No 2* (1972)
Boumphrey, Ian & Marilyn, *Yesterday's Wirral No 4* (1986)
Boumphrey, Ian & Marilyn, *Yesterday's Wirral No 5* (1990)
Boumphrey, Ian & Marilyn, *Yesterday's Wirral No 7* (1993)
Cullen, Tom, *Crippen: The Mild Murderer* (1977)
LeNeve, Ethel, *Ethel LeNeve: Her Life Story* (1910)
Smith, *Frederick Edwin, Earl of Birkenhead* (1933)
Wilton, J Oldham, *The Ismay Line* (1961)
Woods, EC & Brown, PC, *The Rise and Progress of Wallasey* (1929)
Young, Filson, *The Trial of Hawley Harvey Crippen* (1920)
Young, Filson, *Famous Trials, Hawley Harvey Crippen -1910-* (1941)

The following newspapers of the day were also referred to:
The Birkenhead News & Wirral General Advertiser
The (London) Evening Express
The Daily Express
The Daily Mirror
The Wallasey & Wirral Chronical
The Wallasey News

OUR BEST ATTENTION
Jane Tulloch

Our Best Attention by Jane Tulloch is the story of a department store in Edinburgh and its staff in the 1970s. Each chapter tells the story of a different character and the tale skilfully weaves together their different stories in a year of unforgettable events.

THE MAN FROM OUTREMER
T. D. Burke

The Man From Outremer by T.D. Burke is a swashbuckling tale of treachery and action. Set largely in Scotland at the time of the early Scottish Wars of Independence around 1300 AD, it follows Derwent, a Scottish Crusader-turned-clergyman, and his involvement in the Fall of Acre in Palestine, then as Prior of Roslin in Scotland.

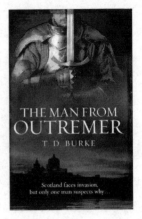

KATIE AND THE DEELANS
Emma Baird

Katie and the Deelans by Emma Baird is the story of Katie Harper and her friends, ordinary teenagers who go to the worst school in the country. Life, however, takes a turn for the extraordinary when Katie and her friends take up magic lessons. Taught by the fabulous Miss D'Azzler and the enigmatic Jazz, Katie and her friends have a lot to learn about life, friendship and love. *Katie and the Deelans* is Comely Bank Publishing's first foray into Young Adult fiction.